A NEW OWNER'S
GUIDE TO
BORDER COLLIES

JG-154

Overleaf: A Border Collie adult and puppy photographed by Isabelle Francais.

Opposite page: Darkwind Sins, owned and photographed by Larry Koval.

The publisher wishes to acknowledge the following owners of the dogs in this book: Becky Babicz, Judy Boles, Ann Bonham, Mrs. J. M. Bradford, Johnathan Browne, Jerri A. Carter, Katherine Choate, Patty Chrisley, Jennifer Collins, Allen Curren, Joan S. Fleming, Jean Freeman, Charles Gray, Teresa Home, Jesse Joad, Larry Koval, Judith Kelly, Terrence Kenney, Duane and Cheryl Loomis, Joanne and John Muzyka, Julie Northshield, Margaret Ouillette, Robyn Powley, Betsy Scapicahio, Peter and Ann Stacey, Dr. Kathy Wells, Joyce and Neil Yaccarino.

Photographers: Judy Boles, Tara Darling, Margaret Diggs, Steve Eltige, Isabelle Francais, Theresa Home, Cheryl Loomis, Alice Pantfoeder, Robert Pearcy, Joe Rinehart Photo, Robert Smith, Judith Strom, Karen Taylor, Michael M. Trafford.

The author acknowledges the contribution of Judy Iby for the following chapters in this book: Sport of Purebred Dogs, Health Care, Identification and Finding the Lost Dog, Traveling with Your Dog, and Behavior and Canine Communication.

The portrayal of canine pet products in this book is for general instructive value only; the appearance of such products does not necessarily constitute an endorsement by the authors, the publisher, or the owners of the dogs portrayed in this book.

T.F.H. Publications, Inc.
One TFH Plaza
Third and Union Avenues
Neptune City, NJ 07753

This book has been published with the intent to provide accurate and authoritative information in regard to the subject matter within. While every precaution has been taken in preparation of this book, the publisher and author assume no responsibility for errors or omissions. Neither is any liability assumed for damages resulting from the use of the information herein.

ISBN 0-7938-2803-1

www.tfh.com

A NEW OWNER'S GUIDE TO
BORDER COLLIES

ROBYN L. POWLEY

Contents

Bred through the years for both form
and function, few Border Collies ever
forget their original purpose.

Who could resist an adorable
Border Collie puppy?

The Border Collie is a hardy working breed, known for his herding abilities.

A loving family dog and guardian, the Border Collie makes a great companion for children.

The Border Collie's athleticism and agility is evident in everything he does.

HISTORY and Origin of the Border Collie

As difficult as it may be to conceive, "man's best friend," the dog, regardless of breed, traces his origin to a common ancestor. Whether the breed is one of the purely decorative and diminutive Toy breeds or a member of the stalwart Working breeds, a dog's ancestry eventually takes him back to none other than the one we know today as *Canis lupis*–the wolf.

The wolf's transition from creature of the forest to mankind's great friend and companion did not happen over night. It began somewhere in the Mesolithic period, which was over 10,000 years ago. At that time, just providing food for self and family and staying out of harm's way was undoubtedly the Mesolithic human's major concern in life. This in itself was no mean feat considering that the use of tools was extremely limited at this stage of human development. There is little doubt that observation of the wolf could easily have taught man some effective hunting techniques to use himself, and many of the wolf's social habits might have seemed strikingly familiar. Wolves saw a source of easily secured food in man's discards. The association grew from there.

Like his forefathers, the noble and steadfast Border Collie stands guard as his flock quietly grazes.

As the relationship developed through the ages, certain descendants of these increasingly domesticated wolves could be advantageously selected to assist in hunting and other survival pursuits. The wolves that performed any function that lightened the load of early human existence were cherished and allowed to breed, while those that were not helpful or whose temperament proved incompatible were driven away.

These wolves-cum-dogs were not only capable of deciding which game was most apt to be easy prey, they knew how to separate the chosen animal from the herd and also how to bring it to ground. These abilities did not escape the notice of man.

Richard and Alice Feinnes, authors of *The Natural History of Dogs*, classify most dogs as having descended from one of four major groups: the Dingo Group, the Greyhound Group, the Mastiff Group and the Northern or Arctic Group. Each of these groups trace back to separate and distinct branches of the wolf family.

The Dingo Group traces its origin to the Asian wolf (*Canis lupis pallipes*). The Greyhound Group also descends from a coursing-type relative of the Asian wolf. The Mastiff Group owes its primary heritage to mountain wolves like the Tibetan wolf (*Canis lupis chanco* or *laniger*). A seemingly odd assortment of breeds that are included in this group, ranging from the upland game dogs to bulldogs and mastiffs, leads one to believe they are not entirely of pure blood. The specific breeds included have undoubtedly been influenced by descendants of the other three groups.

The fourth classification is the Arctic or Nordic Group of dogs which are direct

Border Collie breeders have strived to preserve the breed's natural herding instincts and good temperament.

After hundreds of years of working outdoors, the Border Collie is a hardy dog that quickly adapts to any kind of weather.

descendents of the rugged northern wolf (*Canis lupis*). Included in the many breeds of this group are: the Arctic-type dogs such as the Alaskan Malamute and the Chow Chow, the Terriers, the Spitz-type dogs including Schipperkes and Corgis and the true herding breeds of which the Border Collie is one of the most important and influential.

Almost all of the Northern Group, like their undomesticated ancestors, maintained the characteristics that protects them from the harsh environment of the upper European countries. Weather-resistant coats were of the ideal texture to protect from rain and cold. There was a long coarse outercoat that shed snow and rain and a dense undercoat that insulated against subzero temperatures. These coats were especially abundant around the neck and chest, thereby offering double protection for the vital organs.

Well-coated tails could cover and protect the nose and mouth should the animal be forced to sleep in the snow. Small ears were not as easily frostbitten or frozen as the large and pendulous ears of some of the other breeds. The muzzle had sufficient length to warm the frigid air before it reached the lungs. Leg length was sufficient to keep the chest and abdomen above the snow line. Tails were carried horizontally or up over the back rather than trailing behind in the snow.

This is not to indicate that there were no cross breedings of the types, nor that abilities peculiar to one group may not have also have been possessed by another. In fact, some historians believe that many of the Northern dogs that retain a degree of hunting ability owe this strength to their Asian Dingo-type heritage that is absent from other breeds whose ancestors were not exposed to this admixture. It is also believed that this cross provided some of these Northern breeds with a more refined attitude and tractability.

With the passing of time, humans realized they could manipulate breedings of these evolving wolves so that the resulting offspring became even more proficient in particular areas. While human populations developed a more sophisticated lifestyle, they also thought up new ways in which the domesticated wolves could be of assistance. Customizing the evolving wolves to suit growing human needs was the next step. They became hunting wolves, guard wolves, and herding wolves. The list of useful duties grew and grew.

Romans Classify the Breeds

One can find documentation of controlled breeding practices by Roman writers as early as the first century AD. The Romans had actually broken down the various types of what by then could be referred to as *Canis familiaris*, the dog, into six general classifications very similar to the "variety groups" used as a classification method by the American Kennel Club (AKC) today. Two thousand years ago, Roman writers talked of "house guardian dogs, shepherd dogs, sporting dogs, war dogs, scent dogs and sight dogs."

Descriptions of the shepherd and herding dogs that had undoubtedly descended from the Northern wolf can be found in Roman writings as early as 36 BC. Many of their characteristics are distinctly similar to those of the modern working Collie. Granted, the dogs described were larger and fiercer than what is expected of the modern Collie breeds but in those early days, the flock dogs were as much guardians as they were herders.

The Roman invasion of Britain introduced these flock guardians to the isles where they continued to protect the stock of the settlers as they had on the Continent. The next wave of invaders to enter the British Isles emanated from Scandinavia. With them came another branch of the northern wolf descendants—the Spitz-type dogs. These dogs were typified by their Nordic characteristics—smaller in size than the Roman descendants and distinguished by their black-with-white or sable-with-white markings and frequently by blue eye coloration.

The difference in size provided a more agile dog, the white markings on the dogs' moving parts were particularly useful in a land where daylight hours were short and night work was not uncommon. In the 1500s, Dr. Caius referred to the "Shepherd's Dog" as a distinct breed in his work on the dogs of England. Two hundred years later, in *A General History of Quadrupeds* by Thomas Bewick, engravings of Shepherd's Dogs bear a striking resemblance to both the rough and smooth Border Collies of today.

These workers of the flocks had no specific name, or at least none found its way into print until 1617 when first mention of these "collie dogs" is found in describing the habits of a Scottish bishop. The latter, it seems, was inclined to arrive

Border Collies have been an integral part of ranching and farming in many countries. This cowboy and his buddies take a siesta.

11

for a visit at meal times like "a collie dog." The actual collie name has several explanations: the word "coalley" meaning black; the Welsh "coelius" meaning faithful, or perhaps the the Scottish variety of sheep known as the "colley."

In order to understand the diversity of the British collie dogs in general, and Border Collies in particular, mention should be made here of a formula used by British stockmen dating back into antiquity. These gifted men developed prize livestock guided by an old adage that stated simply, "Horses for courses." That is, one should choose a formula that will produce a horse best suited to the terrain on which the horse will work. This formula was applied to breeding of all animals, including dogs and from it came some of the world's most outstanding livestock dogs.

Considering the kaleidoscopic initial infusion of blood and the subsequent selection on the basis of the terrain on which the dog would work, it should not be difficult to understand the diversity in looks and temperament found in the modern Border Collie.

The old Highland Collie, which figures in the development of the Border Collie, was a large strong dog with an aggressive temperament ideally suited to controlling the wild highland sheep and untamed highland cattle. On the other hand, the Welsh Collie, another ancestor, was small and agile, perfect for herding flocks of small goats and sheep in the sparsely populated mountainous region of Wales.

The latter was far more an "all-round" type of dog with a distinctly more amiable attitude. It was used for a variety of jobs, such as gathering sheep, driving cattle, and guarding property. Above all, the dogs were very interactive with people and highly domesticated.

Some dogs were bred to cover over 100 miles of hilly

The Border Collie's distinctive markings and eye color have set him apart from other breeds. This Border has a typical black-and-white coat and blue eyes.

With the utmost courage and determination, the Border Collie possesses legendary skill as a herding dog.

terrain in a day, subduing large wild ewes. Others were bred for less intensive drive and energy.

The first recorded Sheepdog trial was held in Wales in 1873. The event was won by a Scottish-bred collie-type dog named Tweed. The description rendered was of an agile and compact tricolored dog. In addition to having won the herding trial, Tweed was awarded the day's prize for type.

Herding trials were rapidly established and held regularly throughout the British Isles. Their success influenced initiation of the events in America and Australia as well.

Highly successful at the trials and in the pastures, working Collies became big business, commanding high prices and constant demand. It appears some of the best of them came from the border counties between southern Scotland and northern England.

In 1893, Adam Telfer of Northumberland, England, bred a litter of Collies that contained one puppy who was to become known as Old Hemp. The dog was a breeder's dream, inheriting all of the good points of his sire and dam and none of their bad. He became one of the greatest field trial dogs England had ever known, remaining undefeated from the time

he began trials at one year of age. Hemp worked with uncanny speed and silence. He kept the sheep in full control with his penetrating gaze, which trialers began to refer to as "the eye." The sheep seemed mesmerized by Hemp and followed his directions without hesitation.

The Border Collie's extreme intelligence and eagerness to please have made him one of the most trainable breeds in existence.

Hemp's physical description set the pattern upon which the modern Border Collie breed standard is set: agile and quick, a dog of about 21 inches and 45 pounds, possessing a long, straight coat, black and white in color. His ears were small and semi-erect.

His trial success attracted females from throughout the British Isles and his prepotency for siring excellent workers only increased his fame and desirability. Requests for his offspring came from as far away as Australia, the United States, and across the Continent.

It is said that all modern Border Collies trace back to this astoundingly capable and prepotent sire. His offspring created an entire race of great working dogs whose abilities earned them their own individual name. The Border Collie name was awarded to these outstanding dogs in 1915 by James Reid, secretary of the International Sheep Dog Society at that time.

In England, the success of the breed in herding trials and simply as workers earned the Border Collie the respect of the most demanding herdsmen, and breeding these valuable dogs continued on in earnest even through two world wars, albeit with the severest of handicaps. Many clever and forward-thinking breeders developed through the years. One of the most important was J.M. Wilson, whose dogs became international herding trial champions of note from 1930 through the early 1950s.

Bred through the years for both form and function, few Border Collies forget their original purpose.

One of Wilson's great winners was his Wartime Cap, who traced back many times to Old Hemp and exerted a profound influence upon the breed. The extent of this influence can be seen in the 1965 International Champion Wiston Cap. Wiston Cap is looked upon as having profound influence upon the breed through his outstanding sons and daughters. Wiston Cap's pedigree traced back to Wartime Cap no less than 16 times.

Oddly, though holding a position of utmost respect among stockmen, the Border Collie was not recognized for conformation competition in England until 1976. The first British show champions were from well-known herding lines. Later, imports from New Zealand and Australia arrived.

The blood of these imports blended well with the British dogs and the breed steadily progressed to the point where in 1994 English Show Champion Dykebar Future Glory ("Sky") not only won the Working Group at the famed Crufts Dog Show, but also went on to win Reserve Best in Show. Sky is of half British and half New Zealand breeding.

THE BORDER COLLIE IN AMERICA

The Border Collie was included in the Miscellaneous Class of the AKC as early as 1955 and remained there with little note or support of that category for nearly 40 years. The fanciers of the breed at that time feared full admission to the conformation classes of the AKC would shift emphasis from the breed's legendary working ability to appearance alone.

Many among the Border Collie fraternity in the United States felt a breed standard could be adopted that would reflect the standards of other countries where the breed's working ability had not been compromised by the show ring. The group turned to veterans of the breed in Australia, New Zealand, and Great Britain for support.

Judy Vos, an internationally respected New Zealand breeder and judge, calmed fears of the breed becoming purely ornamental by reporting the Border Collie had been in the show ring in New Zealand since 1927, and there had been no discernible ill effects on the breed as far as his ability to work. Proof of this was shown in 1996 when Ma Biche of Whenway, a daughter of New Zealand Ch./British Show Ch. Clan-Abby Blue Aberdoone, became the first show bred Border Collie to be registered on merit by the International Sheep Dog Society (ISDS).

Through the efforts of those interested in seeing the Border Collie take his place in the show rings of America, a breed standard was drafted and submitted to the AKC for approval in November of 1994. That standard became effective in January of 1995 and the breed was given Herding Group designation on October 1, 1995. The AKC named the Border Collie Society of America the breed's official parent club.

The first AKC champion of record was the author's New Zealand import, Clan-Abby To-Hell-And-Back, with the first Herding Group win being awarded to an Australian import, Ch. Clan-Abby The Wizard of Oz owned by Warren and Carol Rice.

Australian and New Zealand breeders have greatly influenced the evolution of the Border Collie. Aus. Ch. Kennoway Bill Bailey is pictured winning Reserve Best in Show.

On March 23, 1997, an Australian import, Ch. Nahrof First Edition, achieved the first AKC all-breed Best in Show. This historic winner was owned by Anne Marie Silverton and Lauren Somers.

CHARACTERISTICS of the Border Collie

I t is highly unlikely that there are many who haven't heard of the Border Collie's legendary intelligence. Those who may not have experienced it first hand have undoubtedly read about the breed or seen one of the many television documentaries extolling the breed's vast capacity to learn. Border Collies appear in movies, television shows, music videos, and on commercials, all showing the breed's famed "smarts." At dog shows they wow audiences in a myriad of ways, always making the difficult look easy. In fact, the top-winning obedience dog in AKC history is a Border Collie, OTCh. Heelalong Chimney Sweep, UDX.

Carefully consider the responsibilities of dog ownership before taking a Border Collie puppy home.

It is this intelligence that draws people to the breed that can become the hardest part of living with a Border Collie. As a breed they are inventive and you can rest assured they will build on anything you teach them.

Far too many prospective owners, impressed by what they see or read about the Border Collie, dash off to find a litter of puppies from which they can select their canine genius. What they find are adorable little youngsters ready to frolic with the world.

But beware, all puppies are picture-postcard cuddly and cute, and Border Collie puppies are no exception. There is nothing more seductive than a litter of fluffy little puppies, nestled together sound asleep, one on top of the other. But in addition to being cute, puppies are living, breathing, and very mischievous little creatures and they are entirely dependent upon their human owner for everything once they leave their mother and littermates. Furthermore, the fluffy and dependent

Border Collies can do almost anything! The breed's intelligence and dexterity make him very easy to train for obedience or agility trials.

Border Collie puppy quickly becomes a bundle of activity whose adolescent hormones continuously rage and inspire relentless curiosity and activity.

Buying a dog, especially a Border Collie, before someone is absolutely sure they want to make that commitment can be a serious mistake. The prospective dog owner must clearly understand the amount of time and work involved in simple dog ownership. Failure to understand the extent of commitment that dog ownership involves is one of the primary reasons there are so many unwanted canines that are forced to have their lives end in an animal shelter. In the case of a Border Collie, the intellect of the breed actually requires more time

19

A wonderful family dog, the Border Collie's enthusiasm and amiability qualify him as a great companion for children. and exertion from owners than what might be required from breeds that are less gifted. The Border Collie cannot be left to his own devices or to live his life in the backyard.

Before anyone contemplates the purchase of any dog, there are some very important conditions that must be considered. One of the first important questions that must be answered is whether or not the person who will ultimately be responsible for the dog's care and well being actually wants a dog.

If the prospective dog owner lives alone, all he or she needs do is be sure that there is a strong desire to make the necessary commitment dog ownership entails. In the case of family households, it is vital that the person who will ultimately be responsible for the dog's care really wants a dog.

In the average household, mothers, even working mothers, are most often given the additional responsibility of caring for the family pets. Irrespective of the fact that nowadays mothers are also out in the workplace, all too often they are saddled with the additional chores of feeding and trips to the veterinary hospital with what was supposed to be a family project.

Pets are a wonderful method of teaching children responsibility but it should be remembered that the enthusiasm that inspires children to promise anything in order to have a new puppy may quickly wane. Who will take care of the puppy once the novelty wears off? Does that person want a dog?

Desire to own a dog aside, does the lifestyle of the family actually provide for responsible dog ownership? If the entire family is away from home from early morning to late at night, who will provide for all of a young puppy's needs? Feeding, exercise, outdoor access, and the like cannot be provided if no one is home.

The whole family must be committed to caring for your Border Collie.

Another important factor to consider is whether or not the breed of dog is suitable for the person or the family with which he will be living. Some breeds can handle the rough and tumble play of young children. Some cannot. On the other hand some dogs are so large and clumsy, especially as puppies, that they could easily and unintentionally injure an infant.

Then, too, there is the matter of hair. A luxuriously-coated dog is certainly beautiful to behold, but all that hair takes care. In the case of a Border Collie, the prospective owner has the option of either a smooth or rough coat. But be aware that both long- and short-haired dogs shed their coats in the home. Naturally, the longer hair is more quickly noticeable and if not kept after, will deposit itself in every nook and cranny of the household. On the other hand, the shorter hair can be much more difficult to release its hold on what it may be attached to. Both coats need brushing.

As great as claims are for the Border Collie's intelligence and trainability, remember the new dog must be taught every household rule that he is to observe. Some dogs catch on more quickly than others and puppies are just as inclined to forget or disregard lessons as young human children.

CASE FOR THE PUREBRED DOG

As previously mentioned, all puppies are cute. Not all puppies grow up to be particularly attractive adults. What is considered beautiful by one person is not necessarily seen as attractive by another. It is almost impossible to determine what a mixed breed puppy will look like as an adult. Nor will it be possible to determine if the mixed breed puppy's temperament is suitable for the person or family who wishes to own him. If the puppy grows up to be too big, too hairy, or too active for the owner, what then will happen to him?

Size and temperament can vary to a degree even within any purebred breed. Granted, there are all the acceptable variations within the Border Collie spectrum. Still, selective breeding over many generations has produced dogs giving the would-be owner reasonable assurance of what the purebred Border Collie puppy will look and act like as an adult. The Border Collie is never going to be as lethargic as a Basset Hound, no matter where he may fall on the temperament spectrum. Nor will a Border Collie ever be as small as a Chihuahua or as large as a Great Dane. There are certain givens. Expect your Border Collie to be nothing more and nothing less.

A person who wants a dog to go along on those morning jogs or long distance runs is not going to be particularly happy with a lethargic or short-legged breed. Nor is the fastidious

The Border Collie thrives on exercise and is happiest when working or playing outdoors.

housekeeper, whose picture of the ideal dog is one that lies quietly at the feet of his master by the hour and never sheds, going to be particularly happy with the shaggy dog whose temperament is reminiscent of a hurricane.

Purebred puppies grow up looking pretty much like their adult relatives and, by and large, they will behave pretty much like the rest of their family. Any dog, mixed breed or not, has the potential to be a loving companion.

The Border Collie's natural athleticism is evident in everything he does. Frisbee™ competition is just one of the activities in which the Border Collie can excel.

No surprises here! The Border Collie puppy should look like his parents, only smaller. Seven-week-old Penelope Blue with owner Allen Curren.

However, a purebred dog offers reasonable insurance that he will not only suit the owner's lifestyle but the person's esthetic demands as well.

WHO SHOULD OWN A BORDER COLLIE?

Just as a prospective buyer should have a check list to lead him or her to a responsible breeder, so do good breeders have a list of qualifications for the buyer.

1. The buyer must have a fenced yard or be willing to provide his Border Collie with the amount of on-leash exercise that this particular breed requires.

2. The Border Collie owner must have TIME. This is not a breed that is appropriate for anyone in need of instant gratification, or whose life is already completely filled with other responsibilities. It takes time to provide the necessary training, stimulation, and human companionship that this breed requires.

3. The dog cannot be made to live exclusively outdoors with little human contact.

4. Children should be old enough to be able to handle a Border Collie puppy's rambunctious attitude.

The Border Collie loves the outdoors and can accompany his family on any outing.

The Border Collie flourishes when he is able to put his energy and talents into positive activities. This Border conquers the A-frame in an agility trial.

5. Everyone in the family must want a Border Collie. Both the husband and wife should be interviewed to determine their desire to own a Border Collie.

6. Many people are initially attracted to the Border Collie because of his legendary intelligence. The thought process can be "I am very smart and therefore should have a very smart dog." This sort of reasoning can lead to disaster and is not a sound reason for owning a Border Collie. The intellect of the breed actually requires more time and exertion from owners—not less.

As sturdy a constitution as the Border Collie may have, and as rugged and sturdy as the breed can be, the breed is completely incapable of withstanding being struck in anger. This devastates the Border Collie and if subjected to treatment of this nature on a continuing basis, it can turn even the most amiable youngster into a neurotic and unpredictable adult.

This is not to say the Border Collie owner needs to or should be passive in raising and training his or her dog. On the contrary, a young Border Collie must start understanding household rules from the first moment he comes into your home. What it will take to accomplish this is the aforementioned time, patience, and a firm but gentle and unrelenting hand. Even the youngest Border Collie puppy understands the difference between being corrected and being abused.

Needless to say, the Border Collie owner must be prepared to take care of the breed's coat. The long coat requires more work and in the mature dog, shedding does continue on a semiannual basis. The responsible owner should allow a half hour or so at least once or twice a week for general coat and health care.

CHARACTER OF THE BORDER COLLIE

One of the Border Collie's most admirable traits is his devotion to the people he loves. This, too, however, can have drawbacks. Border Collies can become obsessive and territorial. In many instances, what starts off as natural affection between man and dog winds up with the dog believing that he owns the person. In situations of this kind, the dog may show aggression to those people who try to come between him and the object of his affection, often to the point of biting.

It must be understood that the Border Collie was developed and rigidly selected through the ages for his ability as a herding dog. The breed's natural instinct to perform as a herder does not disappear simply because there are no cattle or sheep around to herd. Even the very mellow Border Collie will exhibit some herding behaviors such as fixing what is referred to as "the eye" on people or rounding up most anything that moves, including people. Most Border Collies are attracted to movement and many are killed chasing cars.

Border puppies may nip at the heels of toddlers, knocking them off their feet. This is often because the young Border Collie does not understand where the young children fit into the "family pack" and are simply attracted to the the little moving feet. This is never "cute" and should be dealt with immediately with a firm "no!" Once this heel-nipping is allowed to happen, it is extremely difficult to stop.

While there are exceptions to the Border Collie's need of a good amount of exercise, someone who only wants a "couch-potato" should look to another breed of dog. The Border Collie has been genetically gifted with intelligence, stamina, and endurance. To expect the breed not to use these characteristics is being terribly unfair to the dog.

Some Border Collies are best described as hyperactive and need intense exercise periods two or three times a day, even in blizzard conditions. In fact, a Border Collie can and will outlast most humans in the exercise department. However, there are many Borders that are very happy with a quick stretch of the legs and 15 minutes of retrieving a ball in the backyard. Again, the tricky part is having the owner be able to meet the dog's need.

There is nothing the Border Collie would rather do than please his owner. "Mist" awaits his next command.

STANDARD for the Border Collie

The standard of the Border Collies is written in a simple and straightforward manner than can be read and understood by even the beginning fancier. However, it takes many years of experience and observation to fully grasp all of the standard's implications. Reading as much about the breed as possible helps a great deal but there is nothing as beneficial as putting yourself in the hands of a dedicated and experienced breeder if you sincerely wish to develop your knowledge of the breed.

Author Robyn Powley with one of her award-winning Border Collies.

OFFICIAL STANDARD FOR THE BORDER COLLIE

General Appearance–The Border Collie is a well balanced, medium-sized dog of athletic appearance, displaying grace and agility in equal measure with substance and stamina. His hard, muscular body has a smooth outline which conveys the impression of effortless movement and endless endurance–characteristics which have made him the world's premier sheep herding dog. He is energetic, alert and eager. Intelligence is his hallmark.

Size, Proportion, Substance–The height at the withers varies from 19" to 22" for males, 18" to 21" for females. The body, from point of shoulder to buttocks, is slightly longer than the height at the shoulders. Bone must be strong, not excessive, always in proportion to size. Overall balance between height, length, weight and bone is crucial and is

The Border Collie should appear athletic and graceful, as well as powerful. Ch. Blacktie Bailey, owned by Teresa Nome.

BEST
FAMILY
CHAPARRAL
KENNEL CLUB
RINEHART
PHOTOGRAPH

more important than any absolute measurement. Excess body weight is not to be mistaken for muscle or substance. Any single feature of size appearing out of proportion should be considered a fault.

Head–*Expression* is intelligent, alert, eager and full of interest. *Eyes* are set well apart, of moderate size, oval in shape. The color encompasses the full range of brown eyes; dogs having primary body colors other than black may have noticeably lighter eye color. Lack of eye rim pigmentation is a fault. Blue eyes are a fault except in merles, where one or both, or part of one or both eyes may be blue. *Ears* are of medium size, set well apart, carried erect and/or semi-erect (varying from ¼ to ¾ of the ear erect). The tips may fall forward or outward to the side. Ears are sensitive and mobile. *Skull* is broad with occiput not pronounced. Skull and foreface approximately equal in length. Stop moderate, but distinct. Muzzle moderately short, strong and blunt, tapering to nose. The underjaw

The Border Collie's ears may be carried erect or semi-erect.

is strong and well-developed. Nose color matches the primary body color. Nostrils are well developed. A snipy muzzle is a fault. *Bite*: Teeth and jaws are strong, meeting in a scissors bite.

Neck, Topline, Body–*Neck* is of good length, strong and muscular, slightly arched and broadening to shoulders. *Topline* is level, with slight arch over the loins. *Body* is athletic in appearance. Chest is deep, moderately broad, showing great lung capacity. Brisket reaching to the point of the elbow. Rib cage well sprung. Loins moderately deep, muscular, slightly arched with no tuck-up. Croup gradually sloped downward. *Tail* is set low. It is moderately long, bone reaching at least to the hock. It may have an upward swirl to the tip. While

A Border Collie's eyes are usually brown, but one or both may be blue. Darkwind's Valhalla has a blue and a brown eye.

concentrating at a given task, the tail is carried low and used for balance. In excitement it may rise level with the back. A gay tail is a fault.

Forequarters—Forelegs well-boned and parallel when viewed from front, pasterns slightly sloping when viewed from side. The shoulders are long and well-angulated to the upper arm. The elbows are neither in nor out. Dewclaws may be removed. Feet are compact, oval in shape, pads deep and strong, toes moderately arched and close together.

Hindquarters—Broad and muscular, in profile sloping gracefully to set of tail. The thighs are long, broad, deep and muscular, with well-turned stifles and strong hocks, well let

Keen, alert, curious, eager—the Border Collie's expression should show intelligence within.

down. When viewed from the rear, hind legs are well-boned, straight and parallel or are very slightly cowhocked. Dewclaws may be removed. Feet are compact, oval in shape, pads deep and strong, toes moderately arched and close together. Nails are short and strong.

Coat—Two varieties are permissible, both having soft, dense, weather resistant double coat. In puppies, the coat is short, soft, dense and water resistant, becoming the undercoat in adult dogs. The *rough coat* is medium to long, texture from flat to slightly wavy. Short and smooth coat on face. Forelegs feathered. Rear pasterns may have coat trimmed short. With advancing age, coats may become very wavy and are not faulted. The *smooth coat* is short over entire body. May have feathering on forelegs and fuller coat on chest.

Color—The Border Collie appears in many colors, with various combinations of patterns and markings. The most common color is black with or without the traditional white blaze, collar, stockings and tail tip, with or without tan points. However, a variety of primary body colors is permissible. The sole exception being all white. Solid color, bi-color, tri-color, merle and sable dogs are judged equally with dogs having traditional markings. Color and markings are always secondary to physical evaluation and gait.

Gait—The Border Collie is an agile dog, able to suddenly change speed and direction without loss of balance and grace. Endurance is his trademark. His trotting gait is free, smooth and tireless, with minimum lift of feet. The topline does not shift as he conveys an effortless glide. He moves with great stealth, strength and stamina. When viewed from the side, the stride should cover maximum ground, with minimum speed. Viewed from the front, the action is forward and true, without weakness in shoulders, elbows or pasterns. Viewed from behind, the quarters thrust with drive and flexibility, with hocks moving close together but never touching. Any deviation from a sound-moving dog is a fault. In final assessment, gait is an essential factor, confirming physical evaluation.

Ranger U.D., owned by Duane Loomis, is an excellent example of a smooth-coated Border Collie.

Temperament—The Border Collie is intelligent, alert and responsive. Affectionate towards friends, he may be sensibly reserved towards strangers and therefore makes an excellent watchdog. An intensive worker while herding, he is eager to learn and to please, and thrives on human companionship. Any tendencies toward viciousness or extreme shyness are serious faults.

Faults—Any deviation from the foregoing should be considered a fault, the seriousness of the fault depending upon the extent of the deviation.

Approved Date: January 10, 1995
Effective Date: April 30, 1995

SELECTING the Right Border Collie for You

Once the prospective Border Collie owner satisfactorily answers all the questions relating to responsible ownership, he or she will undoubtedly want to rush out and purchase a puppy immediately. Take care—do not act in haste. The purchase of any dog is an important step since a well-cared-for dog will live with you for many years. In the case of a Border Collie, this could easily be 12, 14, or perhaps even 15 years. You will undoubtedly want the dog you live with for that length of time to be one you will enjoy.

It is extremely important that your Border is purchased from a breeder who has earned a reputation over the years for consistently producing dogs that are mentally and physically sound. There are always those who are ready and willing to exploit a breed for financial gain with no thought given to its health or welfare, or to the homes in which the dogs will be living.

It is easy to fall in love with an adorable Border Collie, but make sure you educate yourself about the responsibilities of dog ownership before taking one home.

The only way a breeder can earn a reputation for quality is through a well-thought-out breeding program in which rigid selectivity is imposed. Selective breeding is aimed at maintaining the virtues of a breed and eliminating genetic weaknesses. This process is time consuming and costly. Therefore, responsible Border Collie breeders protect their investment by providing the utmost in prenatal care for their brood matrons and maximum care and nutrition for the resulting offspring. Once the puppies arrive, the knowledgeable breeder initiates a well-thought-out socialization process.

The first question a prospective owner should ask a breeder is "What is the number one characteristic you breed for?" Deal only with those breeders that answer "Good temperament." Anything else is the first step on the road to tragedy.

The buyer should also ask what the breeder does with his or her Borders. This will give some insight on the characteristics

that breeder is selecting for, such as aggression, energy level, drive, eye, bite, and so forth. It will also tell the buyer which breeders actually live with their own dogs as pets—always a good sign.

The best puppies are born and raised in close proximity with their human family. At Darkwind, our puppies are whelped in the bedroom closet and kept close to us from the very beginning of their lives. They are imprinted with the scents and sounds of humans. Puppies born in a barn and given few opportunities to be with humans seldom achieve their full potential as companions.

The buyer should look for cleanliness in both the dogs and the areas in which the dogs are kept. Cleanliness is the first clue that tells you how much the breeder cares about the dogs he or she owns.

The governing kennel clubs in the different countries of the world maintain lists of local breed clubs and breeders that can lead a prospective dog buyer to responsible breeders of quality stock. Should you not be sure of where to contact a respected breeder in your area, we strongly recommend

Your Border puppy will have a good start in life if his parents are healthy and well adjusted. Litter bred by Joyce and Neil Yaccarino.

contacting your local kennel club for recommendations.

There is every possibility that a reputable breeder resides in your area who will not only be able to provide the right Border Collie for you, but who will often have both the parents of the puppy on the premises as well. This gives you an opportunity to see first hand what kind of dogs are in the background of the puppy you are considering. Good breeders are not only willing to have you see their dogs but also to inspect the facility in which the dogs are raised as well. These breeders will also be able to discuss problems that exist in the breed with you and how they deal with these problems.

As we have mentioned previously, do not be surprised if a concerned breeder asks many questions about you and the environment in which your Border will be raised. Good breeders are just as concerned with the quality of the homes to which their dogs are going as you, the buyer, are in obtaining a sound and healthy dog.

Once separated from his mother and littermates, the Border puppy will look to you, his owner, to take care of all his needs.

Do not think a good Border Collie puppy can only come from a large kennel. On the contrary, today many of the best breeders raise dogs in their homes as a hobby. It is important, however, that you not allow yourself to fall into the hands of an irresponsible "backyard breeder." Backyard breeders separate themselves from the hobby breeder through their lack of responsibility to use their stock to its full potential. A hobby breeder's dogs find their way into the show and obedience ring or participate in the many and varied pursuits in which the breed excels. What is referred to as a backyard breeder is an individual who simply breeds dogs to sell.

If there are no local breeders in your area, there are legitimate and reliable breeders throughout the country that will appear on the Border Collie club or national kennel club lists. These established breeders are accustomed to safely shipping puppies to different states, even different countries.

Always check references of these breeders and do not hesitate to ask for documentation of their answers. The breeder will undoubtedly have as many questions for you as you will have for him or her. When you call a far away breeder, call at a reasonable hour, and expect to have a lengthy conversation. The amount of money you invest in a satisfying telephone conversation may save you huge veterinary costs and a great deal of unhappiness.

HEALTH CONCERNS

All breeds of dogs have genetic problems that must be paid attention to and just because a male and female do not show evidence of problems, this does not mean their pedigrees are free of something that might be entirely incapacitating. Again, rely upon recommendations from national kennel clubs or local breed clubs when looking for a breeder.

Breed health problems can only be eliminated by thoughtful breeders who are willing to breed selectively and discuss these issues openly. It is important that you ask the breeder you are considering about the following:

Hip Dysplasia—a degenerative deformity of the hip joint that causes lameness and in advanced cases, extreme pain.

Collie Eye Anomaly—Progressive Retinal Atrophy and Persistent Pupillary Membrane are just a few eye problems found in Border Collies. All breeding stock should be tested annually and certified clear by the Canine Eye Research Foundation (CERF) in the US or by a veterinary ophthalmologist in other countries. Puppies should be eye tested before 12 weeks of age.

Epilepsy—a brain disorder causing seizures.

Ceroid Lipofuscinosis (storage disease)—results in a buildup of waste materials in the body especially in nerve cells. It is always fatal.

Deafness—both unilateral and bilateral. The latter can be extremely difficult to detect without resorting to a bilateral auditory evoked response (BAER) testing.

Nowadays, many breeders are also certifying elbows and thyroid function with the Orthopedic Foundation for Animals (OFA). Again, it is important that both the buyer and the seller ask questions. This is not to say the puppy you buy or his relatives will be afflicted with any of the above, but concerned breeders are well aware of their presence in the breed.

The gifted breeder uses all the answers you give to match the right puppy with the right home. Households with boisterous children generally need a puppy that differs from the one appropriate for a sedate single adult. The time you spend in making the right selection ensures you of getting the right Border Collie for your lifestyle.

If questions are not asked, information is not received. We would be highly suspect of a person who is willing to sell you a Border Collie with "no questions asked."

A pup's personality will be evident when you watch him play with his littermates.

RECOGNIZING A HEALTHY PUPPY

Most breeders do not release their puppies until the puppies have been given their "puppy shots." Normally, this is at about seven to nine weeks of age. At this age they will bond extremely well with their new owners and the puppies are entirely weaned. Nursing puppies receive temporary immunization from their

mother. Once weaned, however, a puppy is highly susceptible to many infectious diseases that can be transmitted via the hands and clothing of people. Therefore, it behooves you to make sure your puppy is fully inoculated before he leaves his home environment and to know when any additional inoculations should be given.

Above all, the Border Collie puppy you buy should be a happy bouncy extrovert. The worst thing you could possibly do is buy a shy shrinking-violet puppy or one that appears sick and listless because you feel sorry for him. Doing this will undoubtedly lead to heartache and difficulty, to say nothing of the veterinary costs that you may incur in getting the puppy well.

If at all possible, take the puppy you are interested in away from his littermates into another room or another part of the kennel. The smells will remain the same for the puppy so he should still feel secure and maintain his outgoing personality, but it will give you an opportunity to inspect the puppy more closely. A healthy little Border puppy will be strong and sturdy to the touch, never bony, or on the other hand, obese and bloated. The inside of the puppy's ears should be pink and clean. Dark discharge or a bad odor could indicate ear mites, a sure sign of poor maintenance. The healthy Border Collie puppy's breath smells sweet. The teeth are clean and white and there should never be any malformation of the mouth or jaw. The puppy's eyes should be clear and bright. Eyes that appear runny and irritated indicate serious problems.

The Border Collie puppy you choose should be bright-eyed, healthy looking, and interested in the world around him.

There should be no sign of discharge from the nose nor should it be crusted or runny. Coughing or diarrhea are danger signals as are any eruptions on the skin. The coat should be soft and lustrous.

The healthy Border puppy's front legs should be straight as little posts and the movement light and bouncy. The best way to describe a Border puppy's movement is like that of a mechanical wind-up toy with legs that cover considerable ground. Of course there is always a chubby clumsy puppy or two in a litter. Do not mistake this for unsoundness, but if ever you have any doubts, discuss them with the breeder.

MALE OR FEMALE?

It is often thought that a spayed female makes the best possible pet in any breed. While this may be true of many breeds, it is not necessarily the case for the Border Collie. Female Border Collies can be independent and possessive. These traits make the females excellent working dogs and wonderful mothers that give

Don't let that innocent face fool you! Eight-week-old Darkwind's Valhalla, owned by Patty Chrisley, can get into plenty of mischief if you let him.

their youngsters meticulous care. However, the independence can mean less attachment as a pet. This possessiveness can also lead to territorial tendencies that result in the female trying to dominate the human owner (and succeeding in doing so). She may aggressively try to keep other people away from the object of her affection.

Then, too, females have their semiannual heat cycles once they have passed one year of age. During these heat cycles of approximately 21 days, the female must be confined to avoid soiling her surroundings with the bloody discharge that accompanies estrus. She must also be carefully watched to prevent males from gaining access to her or she will become pregnant.

In contrast, the male Border Collies can often be more mellow and a generally happier fellow to be around. While owners of other breeds find training the male not to "lift his leg" and mark his territory indoors troublesome, Border males are not difficult to correct in this respect.

Unless the dog has a highly developed herding instinct, Border Collie males seldom go wandering. They are far more interested in staying home to watch over their families.

It should be understood that most sexually related problems can be avoided by having the pet Border Collie "altered." Spaying the female and neutering the male saves the pet owner all the headaches of either of the sexually related problems without changing the character of the breed. If there is any change at all in the altered Border Collie, it is in making the dog an even more amiable companion. Above all, altering your pet precludes the possibility of his adding to the serious pet over-population problems that exist worldwide.

SELECTING A SHOW PROSPECT PUPPY

It should be understood that the most any breeder can offer is an opinion on the "show potential" of a particular puppy. The most promising eight-week-old puppy can grow up to be a mediocre adult. A breeder has no control over this.

Any predictions breeders make about a puppy's future are based upon their experience with past litters that have produced winning showdogs. It is obvious that the more successful a breeder has been in producing winning Border Collies over the years, the broader his or her base of comparison will be.

A puppy's potential as a show dog is determined by how closely he adheres to the demands of the standard of the breed. While most breeders concur there is no such thing as "a sure thing" when it comes to predicting winners, they are also quick to agree that the older a puppy is, the better are your chances of making any predictions at all.

It makes little difference to the owner of a pet if his Border Collie is poorly marked or if an ear hangs down a bit. Neither would it make a difference if a male pup has only one testicle. These faults do not interfere with a Border Collie becoming a healthy loving companion. However, these flaws would keep that Border from a winning show career.

While it certainly behooves the prospective buyer of a show prospect puppy to be as familiar with the standard of the breed as possible, it is even more important for the buyer to put his or herself into the hands of a successful and respected breeder of winning Borders. The experienced breeder knows there are certain age-related shortcomings in young

If you wish to show your Border Collie, your breeder can help you pick a pup with potential. At six months of age, Angel has all the makings of a future champion.

Border Collies that maturity will take care of and other faults that will completely eliminate him from consideration as a show prospect. Also, breeders are always looking for the right homes in which to place their show prospect puppies and will be particularly helpful when they know you plan to show one of their dogs.

The important thing to remember in choosing your first show prospect is "cuteness" may not be consistent with quality. An extroverted puppy in the litter might decide he belongs to you. If you are simply looking for a pet, that is the puppy for you. However, if you are genuinely interested in showing your Border Collie, you must keep your head and without disregarding good temperament, give serious consideration to what the standard says a show-type Border Collie must be.

The complete standard of the breed is presented in this book and there are also a number of other books and organizations that can assist the newcomer in learning more about the breed. Anyone wishing to breed or show dogs should fortify himself with as much information as possible.

When selecting a show quality puppy, all the foregoing regarding soundness and health apply here as well. It must be remembered though, spaying and castration are not reversible procedures and once done eliminate the possibility of ever breeding or showing your Border Collie in conformation shows. Altered dogs can, however, be shown in obedience and herding trials and many other competitive events.

There are a good number of additional points to be considered for the show dog as well. When selecting a show quality puppy, look for overall balance, with no obvious faults

Responsible breeders will only breed dogs of the best quality in order to improve the health and temperament of their lines.

according to the AKC breed standard. Even in an eight-week-old puppy, we expect to see good movement, including good foot timing, since according to the standard, gait is of paramount importance when judging the breed. Also critical is the right personality. Look for a puppy that has sparkle and charisma!

Prior to six months of age, you may show your Border in puppy matches to aquaint him with ring procedures.

Border Collies in colors other than the traditional black and white can draw a judge's attention at first glance, however, this is only to be an advantage if the dog is sound in both conformation and temperament. Lastly, we consider markings but only to the extent that they add or detract from the dog. In the author's opinion, traditional symmetrical markings are simply icing on the cake.

PUPPY OR ADULT?

A young puppy is not your only option when contemplating the purchase of a Border Collie. In some cases an adult dog or older puppy may be just the answer. It certainly eliminates the trials and tribulations of housebreaking, chewing, and the myriad of other problems associated with a very young puppy. The greatest advantages in purchasing an adult or older puppy, however, are that the size of the older Border as well as the energy level, drive, and herding instinct are all well established. All this makes for a better job in determining compatibility.

There is a national rescue organization called the North American Border Collie Rescue Network that can be a great source for obtaining a Border Collie. There are many people doing rescue work on an individual basis as well. Many wonderful Border Collies are given to rescues each year because their owners did not understand the work and effort that would be required. It is important, however, to use the same sense of discrimination and ask lots of questions before adopting a Border through rescue. One should ask how the dog was treated, and if there is any history of aggression, as well as ask questions regarding drive and energy.

A few adult Border Collies may have become set in their ways and while you may not have to contend with the problems of puppyhood, do realize there is the occasional adult that may have developed habits that do not entirely suit you or your lifestyle. Arrange to bring an adult Border into your home on a trial basis. That way neither you nor the dog will be obligated should either of you decide you are incompatible.

IMPORTANT PAPERS

The purchase of any purebred dog entitles you to three very important documents: a health record containing an inoculation list, a copy of the dog's pedigree, and the registration certificate.

Health Record

Most Border Collie breeders have initiated the necessary inoculation series for their puppies by the time they are eight weeks of age. These inoculations protect the puppies against hepatitis, leptospirosis, distemper, and canine parvovirus. In most cases, rabies inoculations are not given until a puppy is four months of age or older.

There is a set series of inoculations developed to combat these infectious diseases and it is extremely important that you obtain a record of the shots your puppy has been given and the dates upon which the shots were administered. In this way, the veterinarian you choose will be able to continue on with the appropriate inoculation series as needed.

Pedigree

The pedigree is your dog's "family tree." The breeder must supply you with a copy of this document authenticating your puppy's ancestors back to at least the third generation. All purebred dogs have a pedigree. The pedigree does not imply that a dog is of show

It's too early to evaluate this puppy's show potential, but even if he does have faults, he'll still make a wonderful pet.

Proper socialization with parents and littermates is important for a pup to learn how to interact with other dogs later in life. Puppy Claire gives her dad Taz a big kiss.

quality. It is simply a chronological list of ancestors.

Registration Certificate
The registration certificate is the canine world's "birth certificate." This certificate is issued by a country's governing kennel club. When you transfer the ownership of your Border Collie from the breeder's name to your own name, the transaction is entered on this certificate and once mailed to the kennel club, it is permanently recorded in their computerized files. Keep all these documents in a safe place as you will need them when you visit your veterinarian or should you ever wish to breed or show your Border.

DIET SHEET
Your Border Collie is the happy healthy puppy he is because the breeder has been carefully feeding and caring for him. Every breeder has their own particular way of doing this. Most breeders give the new owner a written record that details the amount and kind of food a puppy has been receiving. Follow

these recommendations to the letter, at least for the first month or two after the puppy comes to live with you.

The diet sheet should indicate the number of times a day your puppy has been accustomed to being fed and the kind of vitamin supplementation, if any, he has been receiving. Following the prescribed procedure will reduce the chance of upset stomach and loose stools.

Usually a breeder's diet sheet projects the increases and changes in food that will be necessary as your puppy grows from week to week. If the sheet does not include this information, ask the breeder for suggestions regarding increases and the eventual changeover to adult food.

Dogs can pick up parasites when outside, so make sure your Border puppy has received his proper immunizations before letting him outdoors.

In the unlikely event you are not supplied with a diet sheet by the breeder and are unable to get one, your veterinarian will be able to advise you in this respect. There are countless foods now being manufactured expressly to meet the nutritional needs of puppies and growing dogs. A trip down the pet aisle at your supermarket or pet supply store will prove just how many choices you have. Two important tips to remember: Read labels carefully for content and when you deal with established reliable manufacturers you are more likely to get what you pay for.

HEALTH GUARANTEE

Any reputable breeder is more than willing to supply a written agreement that the sale of your Border Collie is contingent upon his passing a veterinarian's examination. Ideally you will be able to arrange an appointment with your chosen veterinarian right after you have picked up your puppy from the breeder and before you take the puppy home. If this is not possible, you should not delay this procedure any longer than 24 hours from the time you take your puppy home.

I believe I can fly! The confident Border Collie can accomplish anything he sets his mind to.

TEMPERAMENT AND SOCIALIZATION

Temperament is both hereditary and learned. Inherited good temperament can be ruined by poor treatment and lack of proper socialization. A Border Collie puppy that has inherited a bad temperament is a poor risk as a companion, a show dog or a working dog and should certainly never be bred. Therefore, it is critical that you obtain a happy puppy from a breeder who is determined to produce good temperaments and has taken all the necessary steps to provide the early socialization necessary.

Temperaments in the same litter can range from strong willed and outgoing on the high end of the scale to reserved and retiring at the low end. A puppy that is so bold and strong willed as to be foolhardy and uncontrollable could easily be a difficult adult that will need a very firm hand. This is hardly a dog for the owner who is mild and reserved in demeanor or frail in physique. In every human-canine relationship there must be a pack leader and a follower. In order to achieve his full potential, the Border Collie must have an owner who remains in charge at all times.

It is important to remember a Border puppy may be as happy as a clam living at home with you and your family, but if the socialization that began at the breeder's is not continued, that sunny disposition will not extend outside your front door. From the day the young Border arrives at your home you must be committed to accompanying him upon an unending pilgrimage to meet and like all human beings and animals.

If you are fortunate enough to have children well past the toddler stage in the household or living nearby, your socialization task will be assisted considerably. Border Collies raised with children seem to have a distinct advantage in socialization. The two seem to understand each other and in

As long as they are properly introduced, your Border Collie should get along well with other pets.

some way known only to the puppies and children themselves, they give each other the confidence to face the trying ordeal of growing up.

The children in your own household are not the only children with whom your puppy should spend time. It is a case of the more the merrier! Every child (and adult for that matter) that enters your household should be asked to pet your puppy. Your puppy

Take your Border Collie with you wherever you go—the more people he meets the better socialized he will become.

Children and Border Collies have a special bond, and caring for a dog teaches a child responsibility. Justin helps his Border "Chelsea" celebrate her first birthday.

should go everywhere with you—the post office, the market, the shopping mall—wherever. Little Border Collie puppies create a stir wherever they go and dog lovers

will want to stop and pet the puppy. There is nothing in the world better for him.

Should your puppy back off from a stranger give the person a treat to offer your puppy. You must insist your young Border be amenable to the attention of all strangers—young and old, short and tall, and of all races. It is not up to your puppy to decide who he will or will not be friendly with. You are in charge. You must call the shots.

If your Border has a show career in his future, there are other things in addition to just being handled that will have to be taught. All show dogs must learn to have their mouths opened and inspected by the judge. The judge must be able to check the teeth. Males must be accustomed to having their testicles touched as the dog show judge must determine that all male dogs are "complete" which means there are two normal-sized testicles in the scrotum. These inspections must begin in puppyhood and be done on a regular and continuing basis.

All Border Collies must learn to get on with other dogs as well as with humans. If you are fortunate enough to have a "puppy *A family affair! Border Collies are great playmates for energetic children—and vice versa.*

The protective Border Collie is an excellent guardian. This Border has rounded up two guinea pigs and dutifully watches his charges.

preschool" or dog training class nearby, attend with as much regularity as you possibly can. A young Border that has been exposed regularly to other dogs from puppyhood will learn to adapt and accept other dogs and other breeds much more readily than one that seldom sees strange dogs.

THE ADOLESCENT BORDER COLLIE

You will find it amazing how quickly the little ball of fur you first brought home begins to develop into a full-grown Border Collie. Some lines shoot up to full size very rapidly, others mature more slowly. A few Borders pass through adolescence quite gracefully but at about nine months become lanky and ungainly, growing in and out of proportion seemingly from one day to the next.

Somewhere between 12 to 18 months your Border will have attained his full height. However, body and coat development continue on until two years of age in some lines and up to three or four in others.

Food needs increase during this growth period and the average Border Collie seems as if he can never get enough to eat. There are some, however, that experience a very finicky stage in their eating habits and seem to eat enough only to keep from starving. Think of Border puppies as individualistic as children and act accordingly.

With the proper training and socialization, your Border Collie can become a valuable and loved member of the family.

The amount of food you give your Border Collie should be adjusted to how much he will readily consume at each meal. If the entire meal is eaten quickly, add a small amount to the next feeding and continue to do so as the need increases. This method will ensure you of giving your puppy enough food, but you must also pay close attention to the dog's appearance and conditions, as you do not want a Border Collie puppy to become overweight or obese.

At eight weeks of age, a Border Collie puppy is eating four meals a day. By the time he is six months old, the puppy can do well on two meals a day with perhaps a snack in the middle of the day. If your puppy does not eat the food offered, he is either not hungry or not well. Your dog will eat when he is hungry. If you suspect the dog is not well, a trip to the veterinarian is in order.

This adolescent period is a particularly important one as it is the time your Border Collie must learn all the household and social rules by which he will live for the rest of his life. Your patience and commitment during this time will not only produce a respected canine good citizen, but will forge a bond

between the two of you that will grow and ripen into a wonderful relationship.

It's a big world out there for your little puppy! Make sure your Border Collie is properly supervised to keep him safe and out of trouble.

CARING for Your Border Collie

FEEDING AND NUTRITION

The best way to make sure your Border Collie puppy is obtaining the right amount and the correct type of food for his age is to follow the diet sheet provided by the breeder from whom you obtained your puppy. Do your best not to change the puppy's diet and you will be less apt to run into digestive problems and diarrhea. Diarrhea is very serious in young puppies. Puppies with diarrhea can dehydrate very rapidly, causing severe problems and even death.

If it is necessary to change your puppy's diet for any reason, it should never be done abruptly. Begin by adding a tablespoon or two of the new food, gradually increasing the amount until the meal consists entirely of the new product. A rule of thumb is this: You should be able to feel the ribs and backbone with just a slight layer of fat and muscle over them. It is important to remember that once the dog gets fat he will not exercise and will be even more prone to weight gain. A vicious cycle begins.

By the time your Border puppy is one year old you can reduce feedings to one a day. This meal can be given either in the morning or evening. It is really a matter of choice on your part. There are two important things to remember: Feed the main meal at the same time every day and make sure what you feed is nutritionally complete. If you wish, the single meal can be cut in half and fed twice a day. A morning or night time snack of hard dog biscuits made especially for large dogs can also be given. These biscuits not only become highly anticipated treats by your Border but are genuinely helpful in maintaining healthy gums and teeth.

"Balanced" Diets

In order for a canine diet to qualify as "complete and balanced" in the United States, it must meet standards set by the Subcommittee on Canine Nutrition of the National Research Council of the National Academy of Sciences. Most commercial foods manufactured for dogs meet these standards and prove this by listing the ingredients contained in the food on every package and can. The ingredients are listed in descending order with the main ingredient listed first.

Fed with any regularity at all, refined sugars can cause your Border Collie to become obese and will definitely create tooth decay. Refined sugars are not a part of the canine natural food acquisition and canine teeth are not genetically disposed to handling these sugars. Do not feed your Border sugar products and avoid products that contain sugar to any high degree.

Fresh water and a properly prepared balanced diet containing the essential nutrients in correct proportions are all a healthy Border Collie needs to be offered. Dog foods come canned, dry, semi-moist, "scientifically fortified," and "all-natural." A visit to your local supermarket or pet store will reveal how vast an array from which you will be able to select.

Make sure your Border Collie has cool clean water available to him at all times, especially after exercising outside.

The important thing to remember is that all dogs, whether they are Border Collies or Chihuahuas, are carnivorous (meat-eating) animals. While the vegetable content of your dog's diet should not be overlooked, a dog's physiology and anatomy are based upon carnivorous food acquisition. Animal protein and fats are absolutely essential to the well being of your Border Collie. Not all dry foods contain the amount of fat that will keep the healthy Border in top condition. A small amount of animal fat such as bacon drippings or beef trimmings can be beneficially added to the Border Collie's diet particularly during winter weather.

This having been said, it should be realized that in the wild carnivores eat the entire beast they capture and kill. The carnivore's kills consist almost entirely of herbivores (plant-eating animals) and invariably the carnivore begins its meal with the contents of the herbivore's stomach. This provides the carbohydrates, minerals, and nutrients present in vegetables.

Through centuries of domestication we have made our dogs entirely dependent upon us for their well being. Therefore we are entirely responsible for duplicating the food balance the wild dog finds in nature. The domesticated dog's diet must include protein, carbohydrates, fats, roughage, and small amounts of essential minerals and vitamins.

Finding commercially-prepared diets that contain all the necessary nutrients will not present a problem. It is important to understand, though, that these commercially-prepared foods do contain all the necessary nutrients your Border needs. It is therefore unnecessary to add vitamin supplements to these diets in other than special circumstances prescribed by your veterinarian. These "special" periods in a Border Collie's life can include the time of rapid growth the breed experiences in

Border Collies need a consistent and nutritious diet to keep in good health.

The high-energy Border Collie will require a diet that is compatible to his active lifestyle.

puppyhood, the female's pregnancy, and the time during which she is nursing her puppies.

Even when required in these special circumstances, it is not a case of "if a little is good, more is better." Over supplementation and forced growth are now looked upon by some breeders as major contributors to many skeletal abnormalities found in the purebred dogs of the day.

Over Supplementation

A great deal of controversy exists today regarding orthopedic problems such as hip dysplasia that afflict Border Collies and many other breeds. Some claim these problems and a wide variety of chronic skin conditions are entirely hereditary, but many others feel they can be exacerbated by diet and overuse of mineral and vitamin supplements for puppies.

In giving vitamin supplementation, one should never exceed the prescribed amount. Some breeders insist all recommended dosages be halved before including them in a dog's diet because of the highly-fortified commercial foods being fed. Still other breeders feel no supplementation should be given at all, believing a balanced diet that includes plenty of milk products and a small amount of bone meal to provide calcium is all that is necessary and beneficial.

If the owner of a Border Collie normally eats healthy, nutritious food, there is no reason why his dog cannot be given table scraps. Table scraps, however, should be given only as part of the dog's meal and never from the table. A Border that becomes accustomed to being hand fed from the table can become a real pest at meal time very quickly. Also, dinner guests may find the pleading stare of your Border less than appealing when dinner is being served.

Dogs do not care if food looks like a hot dog or wedge of cheese. Truly nutritious dog foods are seldom manufactured to look like food that appeals to humans. Dogs only care about how food smells and tastes. It is highly doubtful you will be eating your dog's food so do not waste your money on these "looks just like" products.

Along these lines, most of the moist foods or canned foods that have the look of "delicious red beef" look that way because they contain great amounts of preservatives, sugars, and dyes. These additives are no better for your dog than they are for you.

Special Diets

There are now any number of commercially prepared diets for dogs with special dietary needs. The overweight, underweight, or geriatric dog can have his nutritional needs met, as can puppies and growing dogs. The calorie content of these foods is adjusted accordingly. With the correct amount

Your Border Collie's nutritious diet will be evident in his shiny coat and overall healthy appearance.

of the right foods and the proper amount of exercise, your Border Collie should stay in top shape. Common sense must prevail. What works for humans works for dogs as well–increasing calories will increase weight; stepping up exercise and reducing calories will bring weight down.

After exercise or play, be sure to keep your Border Collie well hydrated and cool to prevent heat exhaustion.

Occasionally a young Border going through the teething period will become a finicky eater. The concerned owner's first response is to tempt the dog by hand-feeding special treats and foods that the problem eater seems to prefer. This practice only serves to compound the problem. Once the dog learns to play the waiting game, he will turn up his nose at anything other than his favorite food, knowing full well what he wants to eat will eventually arrive. Give your Border the proper food you want him to eat. The dog may well turn up his nose for a day or two and refuse to eat anything. However, you can rest assured when your dog is really hungry, he will eat.

Unlike humans, dogs have no suicidal tendencies. A healthy dog will not starve himself to death. He may not eat enough to keep himself in the shape we find ideal and attractive, but he will definitely eat enough to maintain himself. If your Border Collie is not eating properly and appears to be too thin, it is probably best to consult your veterinarian.

BATHING AND GROOMING

The Border Collie is a natural breed that requires little clipping or trimming. This does not mean the breed needs no coat care at all. Regular thorough brushing and a bath when needed are an important part of keeping your dog clean, healthy, and a pleasant companion.

The easiest way to groom a Border Collie is by placing him on a grooming table. A grooming table can be built or purchased at your local pet shop. Make sure the table is of a height at which you can work comfortably either sitting or standing. Adjustable-height grooming tables are available at most pet outlets. Although you will buy the grooming table when your puppy first arrives, anticipate your dog's full-grown size in making your purchase and select or build a table that will accommodate a fully-grown Border Collie. It is best to use a grooming table that has an "arm" and a "noose." The noose slips around the dog's neck when he is standing and keeps the dog from fidgeting about or deciding he has had enough grooming.

Puppies receive their first nutrients through nursing. After that, it is up to you, the owner, to provide them with a high-quality dog food.

You will need to invest in two brushes: a "pin" brush which has long wire bristles set in rubber for the long hair, and a "slicker" brush which has shorter angled bristles that is best used on the

shorter hair of the head and feet and to help break up mats that may occur. You will also need a steel comb to remove any debris that collects in the longer furnishings. A comb that has teeth divided between fine and coarse is ideal.

Consider the fact that you will be using this equipment for many years, so buy the best of these items that you can afford.

Any attempt to groom your puppy on the floor may result with you spending a good part of your time chasing him around the room. Nor is sitting on the floor for long stretches of time the most comfortable position in the world for the average adult.

When brushing, go through the coat from the skin out. Do this all over the body and be especially careful to attend to the hard-to-reach areas between the legs, behind the ears, and under the body. While the correct Border Collie coat seldom mats or tangles, this can occur during the time when the Border is shedding his puppy coat or if an adult catches burrs

The Border Collie is a breed that requires little clipping or trimming. Regular brushing will keep your Border looking great.

or sticky substances in his longer furnishings.

Should you encounter a mat that does not brush out easily, use your fingers and the steel comb to separate the hairs as much as possible. Do not cut or pull out the matted hair. Apply baby powder or one of the specially prepared grooming powders directly to the mat and brush completely from the skin out.

Nail Trimming

Puppyhood is a good time to accustom your Border to having his nails trimmed and having his feet inspected. Your puppy may not particularly like this part of his toilette, but with patience and the passing of time he will eventually resign himself to the fact that these "manicures" are a part of life. Nail trimming must be done with care in that it is important not to cut into the "quick." Dark nails make it difficult to see the quick which grows close to the end of the nail and contains very sensitive nerve endings. If the nail is allowed to grow too long, it will be impossible to cut it back to a proper length without cutting into the quick. This causes severe pain to the dog and can also result in a great deal of bleeding that can be very difficult to stop.

The nails of a Border who spends most of his time indoors or on grass when outdoors can grow long very quickly. Do not allow the nails to become overgrown and then expect to cut them back easily. If your Border is getting plenty of exercise on cement or rough hard pavement, the nails may keep sufficiently worn down. Otherwise they must then be carefully trimmed back.

Should the quick be nipped in the trimming process, there are any number of blood-clotting

If you brush your Border Collie daily, he will only need a bath occasionally. Penny, owned by Allen Curren, takes her first bath.

products available at pet shops that will almost immediately stem the flow of blood. It is wise to have one of these products on hand in case there is a nail trimming accident or the dog tears a nail on his own.

There are coarse metal files available at your pet emporium or hardware store that can be used in place of the nail clippers. This is a more gradual method of taking the nail back and one is far less apt to injure the quick.

The Wet Bath

Consistent brushing and a wash cloth will keep the Border's coat surprisingly clean, but there are occasions where a full bath may be required. Following the foregoing coat care procedure will all but eliminate the need for bathing a Border Collie more than a few times during the year. However, more frequent bathing is perfectly fine as long as you use a top-quality dog shampoo.

The Border Collie's natural coat is very easy to care for.

On the occasion your Border requires a wet bath, you will need to gather the necessary equipment ahead of time. A rubber mat should be placed at the bottom of the tub to avoid your dog slipping and thereby becoming frightened. A rubber spray hose is absolutely necessary to remove all shampoo residue.

A small cotton ball placed inside each ear will avoid water running down into the dog's ear canal. Be very careful when washing around the eyes as soaps and shampoos can be extremely irritating. A tiny dab of petroleum jelly or a drop of mineral oil in each eye will help prevent shampoo from irritating the eye.

In bathing, start behind the ears and work back. Use a wash cloth to soap and rinse around the head and face. Once you have shampooed your dog, you must rinse the coat thoroughly and when you feel quite certain all shampoo residue has been removed, rinse once more. Shampoo residue in the coat is sure to dry the hair and could cause skin irritation.

As soon as you have completed the bath, use heavy towels to remove as much of the excess water as possible. Your

Border will undoubtedly assist you in the process by shaking a great deal of the water out of his coat on his own.

Brush drying the coat with the assistance of a hair dryer (human or special canine blower-type) will reduce drying time significantly. When using a hair dryer of any kind, always keep the setting on "medium." Anything warmer can dry the coat and in extreme cases, actually burn the skin or hair.

EXERCISE

As discussed previously, it is absolutely impossible to to set hard and fast rules concerning the amount of exercise any Border Collie must have. It depends entirely upon the individual dog but do remember the breed's heritage—the Border was bred to work a full day, every day!

Needless to say, puppies should never be forced to exercise. Normally, they are little dynamos of energy and keep themselves busy all day long interspersed with frequent naps.

Mature Border Collies are not only capable of but are delighted to be jogging companions. They can also be exercised using a special bicycle attachment on a bike. It is important, however, to use good judgment in any exercise program. Begin slowly and increase the distance to be covered very gradually over an extended period of time. Use special precautions in hot weather. High temperatures and forced exercise are a dangerous combination.

The best exercise for a Border Collie, however, is that which it acquires in the pursuit of the many organized activities for which the breed is particularly well suited. Agility, flyball, obedience, and herding activities exercise the Border Collie's mind and body. There is no better way to ensure your Border Collie of a happy and healthy existence.

The Border Collie was bred to put in a full day of work and needs a lot of exercise for his physical and mental well-being.

SOCIALIZATION

It should be understood that as stable as the Border Collie breed is, a young dog that has never been exposed to strangers, traffic noises, or boisterous children could become confused and frightened. It is important

that a Border owner give his or her dog the opportunity to experience all of these situations gradually, with his trusted owner present for support.

Home, sweet home! Every dog should have a place in the house where he can retreat and relax.

Make sure your Border is in a secure place if you must leave him alone for a few minutes. Max waits patiently for someone to spring him from "puppy jail."

HOUSEBREAKING Your Border Collie

Here again is the double-edged sword. Border Collies generally are quick and easy to housebreak. However, if the owner is inconsistent or lackadaisical in his or her approach, the Border gets a mixed message and as a consequence may well suit himself.

Border Collies can be extremely strong willed and will try to assert themselves to become pack leaders–even over humans. Some lines are slow to mature physically and emotionally and this necessitates great patience on the part of the trainer. It is best to begin training at eight weeks of age with clear and consistent messages to the puppy of what the limits are and what is and is not acceptable behavior.

The Border Collie's legendary intelligence can be as much a challenge as an asset. You must establish yourself as pack leader from the beginning of your relationship.

Borders will continually test their owners! A dog that has come to his owner when called for months may suddenly run away or just flat out refuse to obey the command. This testing is especially prevalent during adolescence and it just so happens that most Border Collies are given up to shelters during this adolescent phase.

Living through Border adolescence is not unlike surviving the human teenage years–it does end and Border Collies have a natural desire to please their owners. Adulthood will most often produce a dog that happily cooperates and joins in on any activity.

There is no breed of dog that cannot be trained. It does appear that some breeds are more difficult to get the desired response from than others. In many cases however, this has more to do with the trainer and his or her training methods than with the dog's inability to learn. With the proper approach, any dog that is not mentally deficient can be taught to be a good canine citizen. Many dog owners do not understand how a dog learns nor do they realize they can be breed specific in their approach to training.

Young Border Collies have an amazing capacity to learn whatever you wish to teach them.

Young Border Collie puppies have an amazing capacity to learn. This capacity is greater than most humans realize. It is important to remember, though, that these young puppies also forget with great speed unless they are reminded of what they have learned by continual reinforcement.

As Border puppies leave the nest they began their search for two things: a pack leader and the rules set down by that leader by which the puppies can abide. Too many owners fail miserably in supplying these very basic needs. Instead, the owner immediately begins to respond to the demands of the puppy and Border puppies can quickly learn to be very demanding.

For example, a Border puppy quickly learns he will be allowed into the house because he is whining, not because he can only enter the house when he is not whining. Instead of learning the only way he will be fed is to follow a set procedure (i.e., sitting or lying down on command) the poorly educated Border puppy learns that leaping about the kitchen and creating a stir is what gets results.

If the young Border puppy cannot find his pack leader in an owner, the puppy rapidly assumes the role of pack leader. If there are no rules imposed, the puppy learns to make his own rules. And unfortunately the negligent owner continually reinforces the puppy's decisions by allowing him to govern the household.

Most Border Collies live in a family environment and must conform to the rules of the household.

The key to successful training lies in establishing the proper relationship between dog and owner. The owner or the owning family must be the pack leader and the individual or family must provide the rules by which the dog abides.

The Border Collie is easily trained to do almost any task. It is important to remember, however, that the breed does not comprehend violent treatment nor does the Border need it. Positive reinforcement is the key to successfully training a Border Collie. Always show your dog the right thing to do and be consistent in having him behave that way.

HOUSEBREAKING

The method of housebreaking recommended is the avoidance of accidents happening. Take a puppy outdoors to relieve himself after every meal, after every nap, and after every 15 or 20 minutes of playtime. Carry the puppy outdoors to avoid the opportunity of an accident occurring on the way.

Housebreaking your Border Collie becomes a much easier task with the use of a crate. Most breeders use the fiberglass-type crates approved by the airlines for shipping live animals. They are easy to clean and can be used for the entire life of the dog.

Some first-time dog owners may see the crate method of housebreaking as cruel. What they do not understand is that all dogs need a place of their own to retreat to. A puppy will soon look to his crate as his own private den.

Use of a crate reduces housetraining time down to an absolute minimum and avoids keeping a puppy under constant stress by incessantly correcting him for making mistakes in the house. The anti-crate advocates who consider it cruel to confine a puppy for any length of time do not seem to have a problem with constantly harassing and punishing the puppy because he has wet on the carpet and relieved himself behind the sofa.

Begin by feeding your Border Collie puppy in his crate. Keep the door closed and latched while the puppy is eating. When the meal is finished, open the crate and carry the puppy outdoors to the spot where you want him to learn to eliminate. In the event you do not have outdoor access or will be away from home for long periods of time, begin housebreaking by placing newspapers in some out of the way corner that is easily accessible for the puppy. If you consistently take your puppy to the same spot, you will reinforce the habit of going there for that purpose.

It is important that you do not let the puppy loose after eating. Young puppies will eliminate almost immediately after eating or drinking. They will also be ready to relieve themselves when they first wake up and after playing. If you keep a watchful eye on your puppy you will quickly learn when this is about to take place. A puppy usually circles and sniffs the floor just before he will relieve himself. Do not give your puppy an opportunity to learn that he can eliminate in the house! Your housetraining chores will be reduced considerably if you avoid bad habits in the first place.

If you are not able to watch your puppy every minute, he should be in his crate with the door securely latched. Each time you put your puppy in the crate, give him a small treat of some kind. Throw the treat to the back of the crate and encourage the puppy to walk in on his own. When he does so, praise the puppy and perhaps hand him another piece of the treat through the wires of the cage.

Do understand a Border Collie puppy of eight to twelve weeks will not be able to contain himself for long periods of time. Puppies of that age must relieve themselves often except at night. Your schedule must be adjusted accordingly. Also make sure your puppy has relieved himself at night before the last member of the family retires.

Your first priority in the morning is to get the puppy outdoors. Just how early this will take place will depend much more upon your puppy than upon you. If your Border is like most others, there will be no doubt in your mind when he needs to be let out. You will also very quickly learn to tell the difference between the puppy's "emergency" signals and just unhappy grumbling. Do not test the young puppy's ability to contain himself. His vocal demand to be let out is confirmation that the housebreaking lesson is being learned.

Should you find it necessary to be away from home all day you will not be able to leave your puppy in a crate, but on the other hand, do not make the mistake of allowing him to roam the house or even a large room at will. Confine the puppy to a small room or partitioned-off area and cover the floor with newspaper.

Ride 'em cowboy! Even though most of today's Border Collies are housedogs, few ever forget their roots.

Make this area large enough so that the puppy will not have to relieve himself next to his bed, food, or water bowls. You will soon find the puppy will be inclined to use one particular spot to perform his bowel and bladder functions. When you are home you must take the puppy to this exact spot to eliminate at the appropriate time.

BASIC TRAINING

It is important for Border Collie owners to understand that the breed thrives and grows on learning. The Border has a great capacity to learn and if this ability is not activated in a positive manner by the Border Collie's owner, the dog can and will become incredibly creative in ways that may well test patience beyond one's limits.

Training should never take place when you are irritated, distressed, or preoccupied. Nor should you begin basic training in crowded or noisy places that will interfere with you or your dog's concentration. Once the commands are understood and learned you can begin testing your dog in public places, but at first the two of you should work in a place where you can concentrate fully upon each other.

The "No!" Command

There is no doubt whatsoever one of the most important commands your Border puppy will ever learn is the meaning of "no!" It is extremely important that your puppy learn this command just as soon as possible. One important piece of advice in using this and all other commands—never give a Border Collie a command you are not prepared and able to enforce! The only way a puppy learns to obey commands is to realize that once issued, commands must be complied with.

Learning the "no" command and praise for desired behavior should start the first day of the puppy's arrival at your home.

Young puppies need a lot of exercise, but they also need plenty of rest. This little guy takes a well-deserved nap.

If you are a patient and flexible teacher, your Border Collie can learn any command. This Border gets his instructions during an agility trial.

Leash Training

It is never too early to accustom your Border puppy to his leash and collar. The leash and collar are your fail-safe way of keeping your dog under control. It may not be necessary for the puppy or adult Border to wear his collar and identification tags within the confines of your home, but no dog should ever leave home without a collar and without the leash held securely in your hand.

It is best to begin getting your puppy accustomed to his collar by leaving a soft collar around his neck for a few minutes at a time. Gradually extend the time you leave on the collar. Most Border puppies become accustomed to their collar very quickly and after a few scratches to remove it, forget they are even wearing one.

While you are playing with the puppy, attach a lightweight leash to the collar. Do not try to guide the puppy at first. The point here is to accustom the puppy to the feeling of having something attached to the collar.

Encourage your puppy to follow you as you move away. Should the puppy be reluctant to cooperate, coax him along with a treat of some kind. Hold the treat in front of the puppy's nose to encourage him to follow you. Just as soon as the puppy takes a few steps toward you, praise him enthusiastically and continue to do so as you continue to move along.

Make the initial sessions short and fun. Continue the lessons in your home or yard until the puppy is completely unconcerned about the fact that he is on a leash. With a treat in one hand and the leash in the other, you can begin to use both to guide the puppy in the direction you wish to go. Begin your first walks in front of the house and eventually extend them down the street and around the block.

Your Border Collie will do his best to understand everything you tell him.

The Come Command

The next most important lesson for the Border Collie puppy to learn is to come when called. Therefore, it is very important that the puppy learn his name as soon as possible. Constantly repeating the dog's name is what does the trick. Use the puppy's name every time you speak to him. "Want to go outside, Rex?" "Come Rex, come!"

Learning to come on command could save your Border Collie's life when the two of you venture out into the world. Come is the command a dog must understand has to be obeyed without question, but the dog should not associate that command with fear. Your dog's response to his name and the word come should always be associated with a pleasant

A Border Collie is up for anything, as long as it includes the outdoors. It is up to you to provide your Border with an outlet for play and exercise.

experience such as great praise and petting or a food treat.

All too often, novice trainers get very angry at their dog for not responding immediately to the come command. When the dog finally does come after a chase, the owner scolds the dog for not obeying. The dog begins to associate come with an unpleasant result.

It is much easier to avoid the establishment of bad habits than it is to correct them once set. Avoid at all costs giving the come command unless you are sure your Border puppy will come to you. The very young puppy is far more inclined to respond to learning the "come" command than the older dog who will be less dependant upon you.

Use the command initially when the puppy is already on his way to you or give the command while walking or running away from the youngster. Clap your hands and sound very happy and excited about having the puppy join in on this "game."

The very young Border will normally want to stay as close to his owner as possible, especially in strange surroundings. When your puppy sees you moving away, his natural inclination will be to get close to you. This is a perfect time to use the come command.

Later, as a puppy grows more self confident and independent, you may want to attach a long leash or rope to the puppy's collar to ensure the correct response. Again, do not chase or punish your puppy for not obeying the come command. Doing so in the initial stages of training makes the youngster associate the command with something to fear and this will result in avoidance rather than the immediate positive response you desire. It is imperative that you praise your puppy and give him a treat when he does come to you, even if he voluntarily delays responding for many minutes.

The Sit and Stay Commands

Just as important to your Border's safety (and your sanity!) as the "no!" command and learning to come when called are the sit and stay commands. Even very young puppies can learn the sit command quickly, especially if it appears to be a game and a food treat is involved.

Your puppy should always be on collar and leash for his lessons. A young puppy is not beyond getting up and walking

The Border Collie's dexterity and aptitude make him a natural for obedience and agility. Mist and handler Sarah Davies practice the weave poles.

Herding can be very dangerous for your dog. Your Border Collie must be carefully trained in herding to avoid any serious injury.

away when he has decided you and your lessons are boring.

Give the sit command immediately before pushing down on your puppy's hindquarters or scooping his hind legs under the dog, molding him into a sit position. Praise the puppy lavishly when he does sit, even though it is you who made the action take place. Again, a food treat always seems to get the lesson across to the learning youngster.

Continue holding the dog's rear end down and repeat the sit command several times. If your dog makes an attempt to get up, repeat the command yet again while exerting pressure on the rear end until the correct position is assumed. Make your Border stay in this position for increasing lengths of time. Begin with a few seconds and increase the time as the lessons progress over the following weeks.

Should your young student attempt to get up or to lie down, he should be corrected by simply saying "Sit!" in a firm voice. This should be accompanied by returning the dog to the desired position. Only when you decide your dog should get up should he be allowed to do so.

Do not test a very young puppy's patience to the limits. Remember, you are dealing with a baby. The attention span of any youngster, canine or human, is relatively short.

When you do decide your puppy can get up, call his name, say "OK" and make a big fuss over him. Praise and a food treat are in order every time your puppy responds correctly.

Once your puppy has mastered the sit lesson you may start on the stay command. With your dog on leash and facing you, command him to "Sit," then take a step or two back. If your dog attempts to get up to follow firmly say, "Sit, stay!" While you are saying this, raise your hand, palm toward the dog, and again command "Stay!"

Any attempt on your dog's part to get up must be corrected at once, returning him to the sit position and repeating "Stay!" Once your Border Collie begins to understand what you want, you can gradually increase the distance you step back. With a long leash attached to your dog's collar (even a clothesline will do) start with a few steps and gradually increase the distance to several yards. Your Border must eventually learn the Sit, stay command must be obeyed no matter how far away you are. Later on, with advanced training, your dog will learn the command is to be obeyed even when you move entirely out of sight.

As your Border Collie masters this lesson and is able to remain in the sit position for as long as you dictate, avoid calling the dog to you at first. This makes the dog overly anxious to get up and run to you. Instead, walk back to your dog and say "OK" which is a signal that the command is over. Later, when your Border becomes more reliable in this respect, you can call him to you.

Play and praise are the best training motivators for your Border Collie. Neil Yaccarino tempts Taz with a tennis ball.

The sit, stay lesson can take considerable time and patience, especially with the Border puppy whose attention span will be very short. It is best to keep the "stay" part of the lesson to a minimum until the puppy is at least five or six months old. Everything in a very young Border Collie's makeup urges him to stay close to you wherever you go. Forcing a very young puppy to operate against his natural instincts can be bewildering for the dog.

Play ball! The Border Collie's playful nature makes training fun.

Hand signals in conjunction with verbal commands are very effective when training your Border Collie. Sarah, owned by Margaret Ouillette, practices her down/stay.

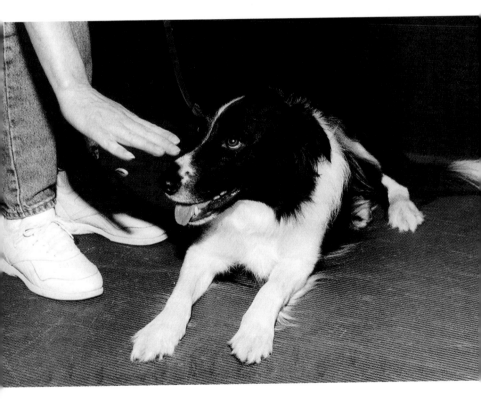

The Down Command

Once your Border has mastered the sit and stay commands, you may begin work on down. This is the single word command for lie down. Use the down command only when you want the dog to lie down. If you want your dog to get off your sofa or to stop jumping up on people, use the off command. Do not interchange these two commands. Doing so will only serve to confuse your dog and evoking the right response will become next to impossible.

The Border Collie's high energy and love of the outdoors make teaching to retrieve a snap! Rosie, owned by Joanne and John Muzyka, fetches her favorite toy.

The down position is especially useful if you want your Border to remain in a particular place for a long period of time. A dog is usually far more inclined to stay put when he is lying down than when he is sitting.

Teaching this command to your Border Collie may take more time and patience than the previous lessons. It is believed by some animal behaviorists that assuming the down position somehow represents submissiveness to the dog.

With your dog sitting in front of and facing you, hold a treat in your right hand with the excess part of the leash in your left hand. Hold the treat under the dog's nose and slowly bring your hand down to the ground. Your dog will follow the treat with his head and neck. As he does, give the command "down" and exert light pressure on the dog's shoulders with your left hand. If your dog resists the pressure on his shoulders, do not continue pushing down, as doing so will only create more resistance.

An alternative method of getting your Border headed into the down position is to move around to the dog's right side

Once your Border Collie masters basic obedience, he can go on to train for more difficult events like agility. and as you draw his attention downward with your right hand, slide your left hand or arm under the dog's front legs and gently slide them forward. In the case of a Border puppy, you will undoubtedly have to be on your knees next to the youngster.

As your dog's forelegs begin to slide out to his front, keep moving the treat along the ground until the dog's whole body is lying on the ground while you continually repeat down. Once your Border has assumed the position you desire, give him the treat and a lot of praise. Continue assisting your dog into the down position until he does so on his own. Be firm and be patient and be prepared for those occasional "I have no idea what you mean" looks your Border student may give you.

The Heel Command

In learning to heel, your dog will walk on your left side with his shoulder next to your leg no matter which direction you might go or how quickly you turn. Teaching your Border to heel will not only make your daily walks far more enjoyable, it will make for a far more tractable companion when the two of you are in crowded or confusing situations.

A lightweight, link-chain training collar is very useful for the heeling lesson. It provides both quick pressure around the neck and a snapping sound, both of which get the dog's attention. Erroneously referred to as a "choke collar," the link-chain collar used properly does *Teaching your Border Collie to heel will make your daily walks much more enjoyable.* not choke the dog. The pet shop at which you purchase the training collar will be able to show you the proper way to put this collar on your dog. Do not leave this collar on your puppy when training sessions are finished. Puppies are ingenious at getting their lower jaw or legs caught in the training chain. Changing to the link-chain collar at training time also signals your Border that he must get down to the business at hand.

As you train your puppy to walk along on the leash, you should accustom the youngster to walking on your left side. The leash should cross your body from the dog's collar to your right hand. The excess portion of the leash will be folded into your right hand and your left hand on the leash will be used to make corrections with the leash.

A quick short jerk on the leash with your left hand will keep your dog from lunging side to side, pulling ahead, or lagging back. As you make a correction, give the "heel" command. Keep the leash slack as long as your dog maintains the proper position at your side.

If your dog begins to drift away, give the leash a sharp jerk and guide the dog back to the correct position and give the "heel" command. Do not pull on the lead with steady pressure. What is needed is a sharp but gentle jerking motion to get your dog's attention.

Your Border Collie must become accustomed to wearing his collar at an early age.

TRAINING CLASSES

There are few limits to what a patient consistent Border owner can teach his or her dog. For advanced obedience work beyond the basics, it is wise for the Border owner to consider local professional assistance. Professional trainers have had long standing experience in avoiding the pitfalls of obedience training and can help you to avoid these mistakes as well.

This training assistance can be obtained in many ways.

Training classes not only are a great place to teach your dog basic obedience, they also provide your Border Collie with an opportunity to socialize with other dogs.

Classes are particularly good for your Border Collie's socialization and attentiveness. The dog will learn that he must obey even when there are other dogs and people around that provide temptation to run off and play. There are free-of-charge classes at many parks and recreation facilities, as well as very formal and sometimes very expensive individual lessons with private trainers.

There are also some obedience schools that will take your Border and train him for you. However, unless your schedule provides no time at all to train your own dog, having someone else train the dog for you would be last on our list of recommendations. The rapport that develops between the owner who has trained his or her Border Collie to be a pleasant companion and good canine citizen is very special—well worth the time and patience it requires to achieve.

VERSATILITY

The Border Collie's keen intelligence, energy, stamina, and desire to please has led to a variety of highly specialized roles. As a herding dog, Border Collies can be trained to trialing standards and to compete in various levels of herding trials. Many Borders are still used as all-around farm dogs and will

Your Border Collie will look to you, his owner, trainer, and best friend, to provide him with the discipline and guidance he requires.

help fetch sheep, goats, and cattle.

In the right hands, it is fairly common for Border Collies to be trained to Obedience Trial Championships (OTCh). The breed excels in all canine sports such as agility, frisbee, and flyball. Borders have wonderful scenting capabilities and can make excellent tracking dogs, and more and more are being used in search and rescue operations.

Because many are so sound in temperament, Border Collies are increasingly used as assistance dogs for the disabled, and many Borders bring comfort to the sick and elderly as therapy dogs. In the United Kingdom, Border Collies are now being used as police dogs, trained to detect both bombs and drugs.

There is actually no boundary to this unique breed's versatility. If the Border Collie has any limitations at all they are usually due to human limitations. We fully expect that a Border Collie will be right along side humans when they set out to explore the universe.

SPORT of Purebred Dogs

Welcome to the exciting and sometimes frustrating sport of dogs. No doubt you are trying to learn more about dogs or you wouldn't be deep into this book. This section covers the basics that may entice you, further your knowledge and help you to understand the dog world.

Dog showing has been a very popular sport for a long time and has been taken quite seriously by some. Others only enjoy it as a hobby.

The Kennel Club in England was formed in 1859, the American Kennel Club was established in 1884 and the Canadian Kennel Club was formed in 1888. The purpose of these clubs was to register purebred dogs and maintain their Stud Books. In the beginning, the concept of registering dogs was not readily accepted. More than 36 million dogs have been enrolled in the AKC Stud Book since its inception in 1888. Presently the kennel clubs not only register dogs but adopt and enforce rules and regulations governing dog shows, obedience trials and field trials. Over the years they have fostered and encouraged interest in the health and welfare of the purebred dog. They routinely donate funds to veterinary research for study on genetic disorders.

Successful showing requires dedication and preparation, but most of all, it should be fun for the dogs and owners alike.

Below are the addresses of the kennel clubs in the United States, Great Britain and Canada.

The American Kennel Club
260 Madison Avenue
New York, NY 10016

(Their registry is located at: 5580 Centerview Drive, STE 200, Raleigh, NC 27606-3390)

The Kennel Club
1 Clarges Street
Piccadilly, London, WIY 8AB, England

The Canadian Kennel Club
111 Eglinton Avenue
East Toronto, Ontario M6S 4V7
Canada

Today there are numerous activities that are enjoyable for both the dog and the handler. Some of the activities include conformation showing, obedience competition, tracking, agility, the Canine Good Citizen Certificate, and a wide range of instinct tests that vary from breed to breed. Where you start depends upon your goals which early on may not be readily apparent.

PUPPY KINDERGARTEN
Every puppy will benefit from this class. PKT is the foundation for all future dog activities from conformation to "couch potatoes." Pet owners should make an effort to attend even if they never expect to show their dog. The class is designed for puppies about three months of age with graduation at approximately five months of age. All the puppies will be in the same age group and, even though some may be a little unruly, there should not be any real problem. This class will teach the puppy some beginning obedience. As in all obedience classes the owner learns how to train his own dog. The PKT class gives the puppy the opportunity to interact with other puppies in the same age group and exposes him to strangers, which is very important. Some dogs grow up with behavior problems, one of them being fear of strangers. As you can see, there can be much to gain from this class.
There are some basic obedience exercises that every dog should learn. Some of these can be started with puppy kindergarten.

CONFORMATION
Conformation showing is our oldest dog show sport. This type of showing is based on the dog's appearance—that is his structure, movement and attitude. When considering this type

of showing, you need to be aware of your breed's standard and be able to evaluate your dog compared to that standard. The breeder of your puppy or other experienced breeders would be good sources for such an evaluation. Puppies can go through lots of changes over a period of time. Many puppies start out as promising hopefuls and then after maturing may be disappointing as show candidates. Even so this should not deter them from being excellent pets.

Usually conformation training classes are offered by the local kennel or obedience clubs. These are excellent places for training puppies. The puppy should be able to walk on a lead before entering such a class. Proper ring procedure and technique for posing (stacking) the dog will be demonstrated as well as gaiting the dog. Usually certain patterns are used in the ring such as the triangle or the "L." Conformation class, like the PKT class, will give your youngster the opportunity to socialize with different breeds of dogs and humans too.

Every dog can benefit from obedience training, especially the Border Collie.

It takes some time to learn the routine of conformation showing. Usually one starts at the puppy matches that may be AKC Sanctioned or Fun Matches. These matches are generally for puppies from two or three months to a year old, and there may be classes for the adult over the age of 12 months. Similar to point shows, the classes are divided by sex and after completion of the classes in that breed or variety, the class winners compete for Best of Breed or Variety. The winner goes on to compete in the Group and the Group winners compete for Best in Match. No championship points are awarded for match wins.

A few matches can be great training for puppies even though there is no intention to go on showing. Matches enable the puppy to meet new people and be handled by a stranger—

the judge. It is also a change of environment, which broadens the horizon for both dog and handler. Matches and other dog activities boost the confidence of the handler and especially the younger handlers.

Earning an AKC championship is built on a point system, which is different from Great Britain. To become an AKC Champion of Record the dog must earn 15 points. The number of points earned each time depends upon the number of dogs in competition. The number of points available at each show depends upon the breed, its sex and the location of the show. The United States is divided into ten AKC zones. Each zone has its own set of points. The purpose of the zones is to try to equalize the points available from breed to breed and area to area.The AKC adjusts the point scale annually.

The number of points that can be won at a show are between one and five. Three-, four- and five-point wins are considered majors. Not only does the dog need 15 points won under three different judges, but those points must include two majors under two different judges. Canada also works on a point system but majors are not required.

Dogs always show before bitches. The classes available to those seeking points are: Puppy (which may be divided into 6 to 9 months and 9 to 12 months); 12 to 18 months; Novice; Bred-by-Exhibitor; American-bred; and Open. The class winners of the same sex of each breed or variety compete against each other for Winners Dog and Winners Bitch. A Reserve Winners Dog and Reserve Winners Bitch are also awarded but do not carry any points unless the Winners win is disallowed by AKC. The Winners Dog and Bitch compete with

Training to compete is not an easy task, but the satisfaction you'll receive when you accomplish your goals is truly rewarding.

the specials (those dogs that have attained championship) for Best of Breed or Variety, Best of Winners and Best of Opposite Sex. It is possible to pick up an extra point or even a major if the points are higher for the defeated winner than those of Best of Winners. The latter would get the higher total from the defeated winner.

The attention and training you give to your Border Collie can only benefit him in the long run.

At an all-breed show, each Best of Breed or Variety winner will go on to his respective Group and then the Group winners will compete against each other for Best in Show. There are seven Groups: Sporting, Hounds, Working, Terriers, Toys, Non-Sporting and Herding. Obviously there are no Groups at speciality shows (those shows that have only one breed or a show such as the American Spaniel Club's Flushing Spaniel Show, which is for all flushing spaniel breeds).

Earning a championship in England is somewhat different since they do not have a point system. Challenge Certificates are awarded if the judge feels the dog is deserving regardless of the number of dogs in competition. A dog must earn three Challenge Certificates under three different judges, with at least one of these Certificates being won after the age of 12 months. Competition is very strong and entries may be higher than they are in the U.S. The Kennel Club's Challenge Certificates are only available at Championship Shows.

In England, The Kennel Club regulations require that certain dogs, Border Collies and Gundog breeds, qualify in a working capacity (herding or field trials) before becoming a full Champion. If they do not qualify in the working aspect, then they are designated a Show Champion, which is equivalent to the AKC's Champion of Record. A Border Collie that earns the title of Show Champion (Sh. Ch.) must pass an ISDS supervised Herding Test to become a champion. Only one Border Collie has earned that distinction to date: Ch. Lochiel Look North or "Nap."

The U.S. doesn't have a designation full Champion but does award for Dual and Triple Champions. The Dual Champion must be a Champion of Record, and either Champion Tracker, Herding Champion, Obedience Trial Champion or Field Champion. Any dog that has been awarded the titles of Champion of Record, and any two of the following: Champion Tracker, Herding Champion, Obedience Trial Champion or Field Champion, may be designated as a Triple Champion.

The shows in England seem to put more emphasis on breeder judges than those in the U.S. There is much competition within the breeds. Therefore the quality of the individual breeds should be very good. In the United States we tend to have more "all around judges" (those that judge multiple breeds) and use the breeder judges at the specialty shows. Breeder judges are more familiar with their own breed since they are actively breeding that breed or did so at one time. Americans emphasize Group and Best in Show wins and promote them accordingly.

The shows in England can be very large and extend over several days, with the Groups being scheduled on different days. Though multi-day shows are not common in the U.S., there are cluster shows, where several different clubs will use the same show site over consecutive days.

Westminster Kennel Club is our most prestigious show although the entry is limited to 2500. In recent years, entry has been limited to Champions. This show is more formal than the majority of the shows with the judges wearing formal attire and the handlers fashionably dressed. In most instances the quality of the dogs is superb. After all, it is a show of Champions. It is a good show to study the AKC registered breeds and is by far the most exciting—especially since it is televised! WKC is one of the few shows in this country that is still benched. This means the dog must be in his benched area during the show hours except when he is being groomed, in the ring, or being exercised.

Typically, the handlers are very particular about their appearances. They are careful not to wear something that will detract from their dog but will perhaps enhance it. American ring procedure is quite formal compared to that of other countries. There is a certain etiquette expected between the judge and exhibitor and among the other exhibitors. Of course it is not always the case but the judge is supposed to be polite, not engaging in small talk or acknowledging how well he knows the handler. There is a more informal and relaxed atmosphere at the shows in other countries. For instance, the dress code is more casual. I can see where this might be more fun for the exhibitor and especially for the novice. The U.S. is very handler-oriented in many of the breeds. It is true, in most instances, that the experienced professional handler can present the dog better and will have a feel for what a judge likes.

In England, Crufts is The Kennel Club's own show and is most assuredly the largest dog show in the world. They've been known to have an entry of nearly 20,000, and the show lasts four days. Entry is only gained by qualifying through winning in specified classes at another Championship Show. Westminster is strictly conformation, but Crufts exhibitors and spectators enjoy not only conformation but

With the proper training, who knows how far your Border Collie can go? Author Robyn Powley and Darkwind friends, both human and canine.

BEST
FAMILY
SANGRE DE CRISTO
KENNEL CLUB

RINEHART
PHOTO

Ch. Korella A Star is Born earned her championship by the age of eight months. Owned and handled by Robyn Powley.

obedience, agility and a multitude of exhibitions as well. Obedience was admitted in 1957 and agility in 1983.

If you are handling your own dog, please give some consideration to your apparel. For sure the dress code at matches is more informal than the point shows. However, you should wear something a little more appropriate than beach attire or ragged jeans and bare feet. If you check out the handlers and see what is presently fashionable, you'll catch on. Men usually dress with a shirt and tie and a nice sports coat. Whether you are male or female, you will want to wear comfortable clothes and shoes. You need to be able to run with your dog and you certainly don't want to take a chance of falling and hurting yourself. Heaven forbid, if nothing else, you'll upset your dog. Women usually wear a dress or two-piece outfit, preferably with pockets to carry bait, comb, brush, etc. In this case men are the lucky ones with all their pockets. Ladies, think about where your dress will be if you need to kneel on the floor and also think about running. Does it allow freedom to do so?

You need to take along dog; crate; ex pen (if you use one); extra newspaper; water pail and water; all required grooming equipment, including hair dryer and extension cord; table; chair for you; bait for dog and lunch for you and friends; and, last but not least, clean up materials, such as plastic bags, paper towels, and perhaps a bath towel and some shampoo—just in case. Don't forget your entry confirmation and directions to the show.

Herding trials help your Border Collie retain his natural instincts and hone his inherent skills.

If you are showing in obedience, then you will want to wear pants. Many of our top obedience handlers wear pants that are color-coordinated with their dogs. The philosophy is that imperfections in the black dog will be less obvious next to your black pants.

Whether you are showing in conformation, Junior Showmanship or obedience, you need to watch the clock and be sure you are not late. It is customary to pick up your conformation armband a few minutes before the start of the class. They will not wait for you and if you are on the show grounds and not in the ring, you will upset everyone. It's a little more complicated picking up your obedience armband if you show later in the class. If you have not picked up your armband and they get to your number, you may not be allowed to show. It's best to pick up your armband early, but then you may show earlier than expected if other handlers don't pick up. Customarily all conflicts should be discussed with the judge prior to the start of the class.

Junior Showmanship

The Junior Showmanship Class is a wonderful way to build self confidence even if there are no aspirations of staying with the dog-show game later in life. Frequently, Junior Showmanship becomes the background of those who become successful exhibitors/handlers in the future. In some instances it is taken very seriously, and success is measured in terms of wins. The Junior Handler is judged solely on his ability and skill in presenting his dog. The dog's conformation is not to be considered by the judge. Even so the condition and grooming of the dog may be a reflection upon the handler.

Usually the matches and point shows include different classes. The Junior Handler's dog may be entered in a breed or obedience class and even shown by another person in that class. Junior Showmanship classes are *Ch. Kiwi-Envoy from Clan-Abby, CDX, owned by Deborah Wood.* usually divided by age and perhaps sex. The age is determined by the handler's age on the day of the show.

CANINE GOOD CITIZEN

The AKC sponsors a program to encourage dog owners to train their dogs. Local clubs perform the pass/fail tests, and dogs who pass are awarded a Canine Good Citizen Certificate. Proof of vaccination is required at the time of participation. The test includes:

1. Accepting a friendly stranger.
2. Sitting politely for petting.
3. Appearance and grooming.
4. Walking on a loose leash.
5. Walking through a crowd.
6. Sit and down on command/staying in place.
7. Come when called.
8. Reaction to another dog.
9. Reactions to distractions.
10. Supervised separation.

Only through experience and training will your puppy learn appropriate behavior.

If more effort was made by pet owners to accomplish these exercises, fewer dogs would be cast off to the humane shelter.

OBEDIENCE

Obedience is necessary, without a doubt, but it can also become a wonderful hobby or even an obsession. Obedience classes and competition can provide wonderful companionship, not only with your dog but with your classmates or fellow competitors. It is always gratifying to discuss your dog's problems with others who have had similar experiences. The AKC acknowledged Obedience around 1936, and it has changed tremendously even though many of the exercises are basically the same. Today, obedience competition is just that–very competitive. Even so, it is possible for every obedience exhibitor to come home a winner (by earning qualifying scores) even though he/she may not earn a placement in the class.

Most of the obedience titles are awarded after earning three qualifying scores (legs) in the appropriate class under three different judges. These classes offer a perfect score of 200, which is extremely rare. Each of the class exercises has its own point value. A leg is earned after receiving a score of at least 170 and at least 50 percent of the points available in each exercise. The titles are:

Companion Dog–CD

Companion Dog Excellent–CDX

Utility Dog–UD

After achieving the UD title, you may feel inclined to go after the UDX and/or OTCh. The UDX (Utility Dog Excellent) title went into effect in January 1994. It is not easily attained. The title requires qualifying simultaneously ten times in Open B and Utility B but not necessarily at consecutive shows.

The OTCh (Obedience Trial Champion) is awarded after the dog has earned his UD and then goes on to earn 100 championship points, a first place in Utility, a first place in Open and another first place in either class. The placements must be won under three different judges at all-breed obedience trials. The points are determined by the number of dogs competing in the Open B and Utility B classes. The OTCh title precedes the dog's name.

Obedience matches (AKC Sanctioned, Fun, and Show and Go) are usually available. Usually they are sponsored by the local obedience clubs. When preparing an obedience dog for a title, you will find matches very helpful. Fun Matches and Show and Go Matches are more lenient in allowing you to make corrections in the ring. This type of training is usually very necessary for the Open and Utility Classes. AKC Sanctioned Obedience Matches do not allow corrections in the ring since they must abide by the AKC Obedience Regulations.

If you are interested in showing in obedience, then you should contact the AKC for a copy of the Obedience Regulations.

The versatile Border Collie can participate in and excel in many different events.

Agility competition tests a dog's coordination and his ability to follow directions. Chloe, owned by Jonathan Brown, maneuvers through the agility tunnel.

TRACKING

Tracking is officially classified obedience. There are three tracking titles available: Tracking Dog (TD), Tracking Dog Excellent (TDX), Variable Surface Tracking (VST). If all three tracking titles are obtained, then the dog officially becomes a CT (Champion Tracker). The CT will go in front of the dog's name.

A TD may be earned anytime and does not have to follow the other obedience titles. There are many exhibitors that prefer tracking to obedience, and there are others who do both.

AGILITY

Agility was first introduced by John Varley in England at the Crufts Dog Show, February 1978, but Peter Meanwell, competitor and judge, actually developed the idea. It was officially recognized in the early '80s. Agility is extremely popular in England and Canada and growing in popularity in the U.S. The AKC acknowledged agility in August 1994. Dogs must be at least 12 months of age to be entered. It is a fascinating sport that the dog, handler and spectators enjoy to the utmost. Agility is a spectator sport! The dog performs off lead. The handler either runs with his dog or positions himself on the course and directs his dog with verbal and hand signals over a timed course over or through a variety of obstacles including a time out or pause. One of the main drawbacks to agility is finding a place to train. The obstacles take up a lot of space and it is very time consuming to put up and take down courses.

Agility is an action-packed sport that is thrilling for the dogs, the handlers, and the spectators.

The titles earned at AKC agility trials are Novice Agility Dog (NAD), Open Agility Dog (OAD), Agility Dog Excellent (ADX), and Master Agility Excellent (MAX). In order to acquire an agility title, a dog must earn a qualifying score in its respective class on three separate occasions under two different judges. The MAX will be awarded after earning ten qualifying scores in the Agility Excellent Class.

PERFORMANCE TESTS

During the last decade the American Kennel Club has promoted performance tests–those events that test the different breeds' natural abilities. This type of event encourages a handler to devote even more time to his dog and retain the natural instincts of his breed heritage. It is an important part of the wonderful world of dogs.

Herding Titles

For all Herding breeds and Rottweilers and Samoyeds.

Entrants must be at least nine months of age and dogs with limited registration are eligible. The Herding program is divided into Testing and Trial sections. The goal is to demonstrate proficiency in herding livestock in diverse

This Border uses the "eyeing" technique to herd ducks. The ability to move stock with such stealth is an inherited trait in the Border Collie.

situations. The titles offered are Herding Started (HS), Herding Intermediate (HI), and Herding Excellent (HX). Upon completion of the HX a Herding Championship may be earned after accumulating 15 championship points.

The above information has been taken from the AKC Guidelines for the appropriate events.

GENERAL INFORMATION

Obedience, tracking and agility allow the purebred dog with an Indefinite Listing Privilege (ILP) number or a limited registration to be exhibited and earn titles. Application must be made to the AKC for an ILP number.

The American Kennel Club publishes a monthly *Events* magazine that is part of the *Gazette*, their official journal for the sport of purebred dogs. The *Events* section lists upcoming shows and the secretary or superintendent for them. The majority of the conformation shows in the U.S. are overseen by licensed

Border Collies excel at agility because of their athleticism and nimbleness. This blue merle Border flies over the bar jump with grace and ease.

Herding competitions are a great place for your Border Collie to show off his considerable skills and be recognized for his contribution to ranching.

superintendents. Generally the entry closing date is approximately two-and-a-half weeks before the actual show. Point shows are fairly expensive, while the match shows cost about one third of the point show entry fee. Match shows usually take entries the day of the show but some are pre-entry. The best way to find match show information is through your local kennel club. Upon asking, the AKC can provide you with a list of superintendents, and you can write and ask to be put on their mailing lists.

Obedience trial and tracking test information is available through the AKC. Frequently these events are not superintended, but put on by the host club. Therefore you would make the entry with the event's secretary.

As you have read, there are numerous activities you can share with your dog. Regardless what you do, it does take teamwork. Your dog can only benefit from your attention and training. We hope this chapter has enlightened you and hope, if nothing else, you will attend a show here and there. Perhaps you will start with a puppy kindergarten class, and who knows where it may lead!

Health Care

Veterinary medicine has become far more sophisticated than what was available to our ancestors. This can be attributed to the increase in household pets and consequently the demand for better care for them. Also human medicine has become far more complex. Today diagnostic testing in veterinary medicine parallels human diagnostics. Because of better technology we can expect our pets to live healthier lives thereby increasing their life spans.

The First Check Up

You will want to take your new puppy/dog in for its first check up within 48 to 72 hours after acquiring it. Many breeders strongly recommend this check up and so do the humane shelters. A puppy/dog can appear healthy but it may have a serious problem that is not apparent to the layman. Most pets have some type of a minor flaw that may never cause a real problem.

Unfortunately if he/she should have a serious problem, you will want to consider the consequences of keeping the pet and the attachments that will be formed, which may be broken prematurely. Keep in mind there are many healthy dogs looking for good homes.

This first check up is a good time to establish yourself with the veterinarian and learn the office policy regarding their hours and how they handle emergencies. Usually the breeder or another conscientious pet owner is a good reference for locating a capable veterinarian. You should be aware that not all veterinarians give the same quality of service. Please do not make your selection on the least expensive clinic, as they may be short changing your pet. There is the possibility that eventually it will cost you more due to improper diagnosis, treatment, etc. If you are selecting a new veterinarian, feel free to ask for a tour of the clinic. You should inquire about making an appointment for a tour since all clinics are working clinics, and therefore may not be available all day for sightseers.

You may worry less if you see where your pet will be spending the day if he ever needs to be hospitalized.

THE PHYSICAL EXAM

Your veterinarian will check your pet's overall condition, which includes listening to the heart; checking the respiration; feeling the abdomen, muscles and joints; checking the mouth, which includes the gum color and signs of gum disease along with plaque buildup; checking the ears for signs of an infection or ear mites; examining the eyes; and, last but not least, checking the condition of the skin and coat.

Your new puppy is very vulnerable and will need to see the veterinarian within 48 hours of his arrival home.

He should ask you questions regarding your pet's eating and elimination habits and invite you to relay your questions. It is a good idea to prepare a list so as not to forget anything. He should discuss the proper diet and the quantity to be fed. If this should differ from your breeder's recommendation, then you should convey to him the breeder's choice and see if he approves. If he recommends changing the diet, then this should be done over a few days so as not to cause a gastrointestinal upset. It is customary to take in a fresh stool sample (just a small amount) for a test for intestinal parasites. It must be fresh, preferably within 12 hours, since the eggs hatch quickly and after hatching will not be observed under the microscope. If your pet isn't obliging then, usually the technician can take one in the clinic.

IMMUNIZATIONS

It is important that you take your puppy/dog's vaccination record with you on your first visit. In case of a puppy, presumably the breeder has seen to the vaccinations up to the time you acquired custody. Veterinarians differ in their vaccination protocol. It is not unusual for your puppy to have received vaccinations for distemper, hepatitis, leptospirosis, parvovirus and parainfluenza every two to three weeks from the age of five or six weeks. Usually this is a combined injection and is typically called the DHLPP. The DHLPP is given through at least 12 to 14 weeks of age, and it is customary to continue with another parvovirus vaccine at 16 to 18 weeks. You may wonder why so many immunizations are necessary. No one knows for sure when the puppy's maternal antibodies are gone, although it is customarily accepted that distemper antibodies are gone by 12 weeks. Usually parvovirus antibodies are gone by 16 to 18 weeks of age. However, it is possible for the maternal antibodies to be gone at a much earlier age or even a later age. Therefore immunizations are started at an early age. The vaccine will not give immunity as long as there are maternal antibodies.

The rabies vaccination is given at three or six months of age depending on your local laws. A vaccine for bordetella (kennel cough) is advisable and can be given anytime from the age of five weeks. The coronavirus is not commonly given unless there is a problem locally. The Lyme vaccine is necessary in endemic areas. Lyme disease has been reported in 47 states.

Distemper

This is virtually an incurable disease. If the dog recovers, he is subject to severe nervous disorders. The virus attacks every

Dogs can pick up diseases from other dogs. Make sure your Border Collie is properly vaccinated before taking him out to meet friends.

tissue in the body and resembles a bad cold with a fever. It can cause a runny nose and eyes and cause gastrointestinal disorders, including a poor appetite, vomiting and diarrhea. The virus is carried by raccoons, foxes, wolves, mink and other dogs. Unvaccinated youngsters and senior citizens are very susceptible. This is still a common disease.

Your veterinarian will put your Border Collie puppy on a vaccination schedule to protect him from disease.

Hepatitis

This is a virus that is most serious in very young dogs. It is spread by contact with an infected animal or its stool or urine.

Good health maintenance throughout your dog's life will keep a smile on her face! Rosie, owned by Joanne and John Muzyka.

The virus affects the liver and kidneys and is characterized by high fever, depression and lack of appetite. Recovered animals may be afflicted with chronic illnesses.

Leptospirosis

This is a bacterial disease transmitted by contact with the urine of an infected dog, rat or other wildlife. It produces severe symptoms of fever, depression, jaundice and internal bleeding and was fatal before the vaccine was developed. Recovered dogs can be carriers, and the disease can be transmitted from dogs to humans.

Parvovirus

This was first noted in the late 1970s and is still a fatal disease. However, with proper vaccinations, early diagnosis and prompt treatment, it is a manageable disease. It attacks the bone marrow and intestinal tract. The symptoms include depression, loss of appetite, vomiting, diarrhea and collapse. Immediate medical attention is of the essence.

Rabies

This is shed in the saliva and is carried by raccoons, skunks, foxes, other dogs and cats. It attacks nerve tissue, resulting in paralysis and death. Rabies can be transmitted to people and is virtually always fatal. This disease is reappearing in the suburbs.

Bordetella (Kennel Cough)

The symptoms are coughing, sneezing, hacking and retching accompanied by nasal discharge usually lasting from a few days to several weeks. There are several disease-producing organisms responsible for this disease. The present vaccines are helpful but do not protect for all the strains. It usually is not life threatening but in some instances it can progress to a serious bronchopneumonia. The disease is highly contagious. The vaccination should be given routinely for dogs that come in contact with other dogs, such as through boarding, training class or visits to the groomer.

Regular checkups are necessary to maintain your Border Collie's good health.

Your Border Collie can pick up parasites like fleas and ticks when outside. Be sure to check his coat thoroughly after playing outdoors.

Coronavirus

This is usually self limiting and not life threatening. It was first noted in the late '70s about a year before parvovirus. The virus produces a yellow/brown stool and there may be depression, vomiting and diarrhea.

Lyme Disease

This was first diagnosed in the United States in 1976 in Lyme, CT, in people who lived in close proximity to the deer tick. Symptoms may include acute lameness, fever, swelling of joints and loss of appetite. Your veterinarian can advise you if you live in an endemic area.

After your puppy has completed his puppy vaccinations, you will continue to booster the DHLPP once a year. It is customary to booster the rabies one year after the first vaccine and then, depending on where you live, it should be boostered every year or every three years. This depends on your local laws. The Lyme and corona vaccines are boostered annually and it is recommended that the bordetella be boostered every six to eight months.

ANNUAL VISIT

I would like to impress the importance of the annual check up, which would include the booster vaccinations, check for intestinal parasites and test for heartworm. Today in our very busy world it is rush, rush and see "how much you can get for how little." Unbelievably, some non-veterinary businesses have entered into the vaccination business. More harm than good can come to your dog through improper vaccinations, possibly from inferior vaccines and/or the wrong schedule. More than likely you truly care about your companion dog and over the years you have devoted much time and expense to his well being. Perhaps you are unaware that a vaccination is not just a vaccination. There is more involved. Please, please follow through with regular physical examinations. It is so important for your veterinarian to know your dog and this is especially true during middle age through the geriatric years. More than likely your older dog will require more than one physical a year. The annual physical is good preventive medicine. Through early diagnosis and subsequent treatment your dog can maintain a longer and better quality of life.

Your healthy Border Collie will be willing and able to learn anything you wish to teach him.

INTESTINAL PARASITES

Hookworms

These are almost microscopic intestinal worms that can cause anemia and therefore serious problems, including death, in young puppies. Hookworms can be transmitted to humans through penetration of the skin. Puppies may be born with them.

Roundworms

These are spaghetti-like worms that can cause a potbellied appearance and dull coat along with more severe symptoms, such as vomiting, diarrhea and coughing. Puppies acquire these while in the mother's uterus and through lactation. Both

hookworms and roundworms may be acquired through ingestion.

Whipworms

These have a three-month life cycle and are not acquired through the dam. They cause intermittent diarrhea usually with mucus. Whipworms are possibly the most difficult worm to eradicate. Their eggs are very resistant to most environmental factors and can last for years until the proper conditions enable them to mature. Whipworms are seldom seen in the stool.

Intestinal parasites are more prevalent in some areas than others. Climate, soil and contamination are big factors contributing to the incidence of intestinal parasites. Eggs are passed in the stool, lay on the ground and then become infective in a certain number of days. Each of the above worms has a different life cycle. Your best chance of becoming and remaining worm-free is to always pooper-scoop your yard. A fenced-in yard keeps stray dogs out, which is certainly helpful.

I would recommend having a fecal examination on your dog twice a year or more often if there is a problem. If your dog has a positive fecal sample, then he will be given the appropriate medication and you will be asked to bring back another stool sample in a certain period of time (depending on the type of worm) and then be rewormed. This process goes on until he has at least two negative samples. The different types of worms require different medications. You will be wasting your money and doing your dog an injustice by buying over-the-counter medication without first consulting your veterinarian.

As a responsible Border Collie owner, you should have knowledge about the medical problems that may affect the breed.

Other Internal Parasites

Coccidiosis and Giardiasis

These protozoal infections usually affect puppies, especially in places where large numbers of puppies are brought together. Older dogs may harbor these infections but do not show signs unless they are stressed. Symptoms include diarrhea, weight loss and lack of appetite. These infections are not always apparent in the fecal examination.

You dog's eyes should be clear and free of any redness or irritation.

Tapeworms

Seldom apparent on fecal floatation, they are diagnosed frequently as rice-like segments around the dog's anus and the base of the tail. Tapeworms are long, flat and ribbon like, sometimes several feet in length, and made up of many segments about five-eighths of an inch long. The two most common types of tapeworms found in the dog are:

(1) First the larval form of the flea tapeworm parasite must mature in an intermediate host, the flea, before it can become infective. Your dog acquires this by ingesting the flea through licking and chewing.

(2) Rabbits, rodents and certain large game animals serve as intermediate hosts for other species of tapeworms. If your dog should eat one of these infected hosts, then he can acquire tapeworms.

Heartworm Disease

This is a worm that resides in the heart and adjacent blood vessels of the lung that produces microfilaria, which circulate in the bloodstream. It is possible for a dog to be infected with any number of worms from one to a hundred that can be 6 to 14 inches long. It is a life-threatening disease, expensive to treat and easily prevented. Depending on where you live, your veterinarian may recommend a preventive year-round and

115

either an annual or semiannual blood test. The most common preventive is given once a month.

EXTERNAL PARASITES

Fleas

These pests are not only the dog's worst enemy but also enemy to the owner's pocketbook. Preventing is less expensive than treating, but regardless we'd prefer to spend our money elsewhere. Likely, the majority of our dogs are allergic to the bite of a flea, and in many cases it only takes one flea bite. The protein in the flea's saliva is the culprit. Allergic dogs have a reaction, which usually results in a "hot

The more time your dog spends outside, the better chance he has of picking up fleas and ticks. Border Collies who live around woodsy areas have greater susceptibility than other dogs.

spot." More than likely such a reaction will involve a trip to the veterinarian for treatment. Yes, prevention is less expensive. Fortunately today there are several good products available.

If there is a flea infestation, no one product is going to correct the problem. Not only will the dog require treatment so will the environment. In general flea collars are not very effective although there is now available an "egg" collar that will kill the eggs on the dog. Dips are the most economical but they are messy. There are some effective shampoos and treatments available through pet shops and veterinarians. An oral tablet arrived on the American market in 1995 and was popular in Europe the

Keeping your Border Collie safely confined when outside will decrease his chances of contracting any internal or external parasites.

previous year. It sterilizes the female flea but will not kill adult fleas. Therefore the tablet, which is given monthly, will decrease the flea population but is not a "cure-all." Those dogs that suffer from flea-bite allergy will still be subjected to the bite of the flea. Another popular parasiticide is permethrin, which is applied to the back of the dog in one or two places depending on the dog's weight. This product works as a repellent causing the flea to get "hot feet" and jump off. Do not confuse this product with some of the organophosphates that are also applied to the dog's back.

Some products are not usable on young puppies. Treating fleas should be done under your veterinarian's guidance. Frequently it is necessary to combine products and the layman does not have the knowledge regarding possible toxicities. It is hard to believe but there are a few dogs that do have a natural resistance to fleas. Nevertheless it would be wise to treat all pets at the same time. Don't forget your cats. Cats just love to prowl the neighborhood and consequently return with unwanted guests.

Adult fleas live on the dog but their eggs drop off the dog into the environment. There they go through four larval stages before reaching adulthood, and thereby are able to jump back

Show your Border Collie you love him by providing him with the best possible health care for a long and fulfilling life.

on the poor unsuspecting dog. The cycle resumes and takes between 21 to 28 days under ideal conditions. There are environmental products available that will kill both the adult fleas and the larvae.

Ticks

Ticks carry Rocky Mountain Spotted Fever, Lyme disease and can cause tick paralysis. They should be removed with tweezers, trying to pull out the head. The jaws carry disease. There is a tick preventive collar that does an excellent job. The ticks automatically back out on those dogs wearing collars.

Sarcoptic Mange

This is a mite that is difficult to find on skin scrapings. The pinnal reflex is a good indicator of this disease. Rub the ends of the pinna (ear) together and the dog will start scratching with his foot. Sarcoptes are highly contagious to other dogs and to humans although they do not live long on humans. They cause intense itching.

Your Border Collie should have a strong, easy stride. Any irregularities in your dog's gait should be reported to your veterinarian.

Demodectic Mange

This is a mite that is passed from the dam to her puppies. It affects youngsters age three to ten months. Diagnosis is confirmed by skin scraping. Small areas of alopecia around the eyes, lips and/or forelegs become visible. There is little itching unless there is a secondary bacterial infection. Some breeds are afflicted more than others.

Cheyletiella

This causes intense itching and is diagnosed by skin scraping. It lives in the outer layers of the skin of dogs, cats, rabbits and humans. Yellow-gray scales may be found on the back and the rump, top of the head and the nose.

To Breed or Not To Breed

More than likely your breeder has requested that you have your puppy neutered or spayed. Your breeder's request is based on what is healthiest for your dog and what is most beneficial for your breed. Experienced and conscientious breeders devote many years into developing a bloodline. In order to do this, he makes every effort to plan each breeding in regard to conformation, temperament and health. This type of breeder does his best to perform the necessary testing (i.e., OFA, CERF, testing for inherited blood disorders, thyroid, etc.). Testing is expensive and sometimes very disheartening when a favorite dog doesn't pass his health tests. The health history pertains not only to the breeding stock but to the immediate ancestors. Reputable breeders do not want their offspring to be bred indiscriminately. Therefore you may be asked to neuter or spay your puppy. Of course there is always the exception, and your breeder may agree to let you breed your dog under his direct supervision. This is an important concept. More and more effort is being made to breed healthier dogs.

Spay/Neuter

There are numerous benefits of performing this surgery at six months of age. Unspayed females are subject to mammary and ovarian cancer. In order to prevent mammary cancer she must be spayed prior to her first heat cycle. Later in life, an unspayed female may develop a pyometra (an infected uterus), which is definitely life threatening.

Spaying is performed under a general anesthetic and is easy on the young dog. As you might expect it is a little harder on the older dog, but that is no reason to deny her the surgery. The surgery removes the ovaries and uterus. It is important to remove all the ovarian tissue. If some is left behind, she could remain attractive to males. In order to view the ovaries, a reasonably long incision is necessary. An ovariohysterectomy is considered major surgery.

Neutering the male at a young age will inhibit some characteristic male behavior that owners frown upon. Some boys will not hike their legs and mark territory if they are neutered at six months of age. Also neutering at a young age has hormonal benefits, lessening the chance of hormonal aggressiveness.

Surgery involves removing the testicles but leaving the scrotum. If there should be a retained testicle, then he definitely needs to be neutered before the age of two or three years. Retained testicles can develop into cancer. Unneutered males are at risk for testicular cancer, perineal fistulas, perianal tumors and fistulas and prostatic disease.

Intact males and females are prone to housebreaking accidents. Females urinate frequently before, during and after heat cycles, and males tend to mark territory if there is a female in heat. Males may show the same behavior if there is a visiting dog or guests.

Surgery involves a sterile operating procedure equivalent to human surgery. The incision site is shaved, surgically scrubbed and draped. The veterinarian wears a sterile surgical gown, cap, mask and gloves. Anesthesia should be monitored by a registered technician. It is customary for the veterinarian to recommend a pre-anesthetic blood screening, looking for metabolic problems and a ECG rhythm strip to check for normal heart function. Today anesthetics are equal to human anesthetics, which enables your dog to walk out of the clinic the same day as surgery.

Some folks worry about their dog gaining weight after being neutered or spayed. This is usually not the case. It is true that some dogs may be less active so they could develop a problem, but most dogs are just as active as they were before surgery. However, if your dog should begin to gain, then you need to decrease his food and see to it that he gets a little more exercise.

Genetic diseases can be passed from generation to generation. It is important to provide preventive health care and screenings to ensure healthy puppies.

DENTAL CARE for Your Dog's Life

So you've got a new puppy! You also have a new set of puppy teeth in your household. Anyone who has ever raised a puppy is abundantly aware of these new teeth. Your puppy will chew anything it can reach, chase your shoelaces, and play "tear the rag" with any piece of clothing it can find. When puppies are newly born, they have no teeth. At about four weeks of age, puppies of most breeds begin to develop their deciduous or baby teeth. They begin eating semi-solid food, fighting and biting with their litter mates, and learning discipline from their mother. As their new teeth come in, they inflict more pain on their mother's breasts, so her feeding sessions become less frequent and shorter. By six or eight weeks, the mother will start growling to warn her pups when they are fighting too roughly or hurting her as they nurse too much with their new teeth.

Give your Border Collie a Nylafloss™ to play with. It will literally floss his teeth while he tugs and plays.

Puppies need to chew. It is a necessary part of their physical and mental development. They develop muscles and necessary life skills as they drag objects around, fight over possession, and vocalize alerts and warnings. Puppies chew on things to explore their world. They are using their sense of taste to determine what is food and what is not. How

If you provide your Border Collie with good dental care throughout his life, he will always be able to flash a healthy smile!

else can they tell an electrical cord from a lizard? At about four months of age, most puppies begin shedding their baby teeth. Often these teeth need some help to come out and make way for the permanent teeth. The incisors (front teeth) will be replaced first. Then, the adult canine or fang teeth erupt. When the baby tooth is not shed before the permanent tooth comes in, veterinarians call it a retained deciduous tooth. This condition will often cause gum infections by trapping hair and debris between the permanent tooth and the retained baby tooth. Nylafloss® is an excellent device for puppies to use. They can toss it, drag it, and chew on the many surfaces it presents. The baby teeth can catch in the nylon material, aiding in their removal. Puppies that have adequate chew toys will have less destructive behavior, develop more physically, and have less chance of retained deciduous teeth.

During the first year, your dog should be seen by your veterinarian at regular intervals. Your veterinarian will let you know when to bring in your puppy for vaccinations and parasite examinations. At each visit, your veterinarian should inspect the lips, teeth, and

Safe chew toys are excellent tools to relieve your Border Collie's need to chew and to keep his teeth occupied.

Your dog's oral care is just as important to his overall health as his nutritional needs. mouth as part of a complete physical examination. You should take some part in the maintenance of your dog's oral health. You should examine your dog's mouth weekly throughout his first year to make sure there are no sores, foreign objects, tooth problems, etc. If your dog drools excessively, shakes its head, or has bad breath, consult your veterinarian. By the time your dog is six months old, the permanent teeth are all in and plaque can start to accumulate on the tooth surfaces. This is when your dog needs to develop good dental-care habits to prevent calculus build-up on its teeth. Brushing is best. That is a fact that cannot be denied. However, some dogs do not like their teeth brushed regularly, or you may not be able to accomplish the task. In that case, you should consider a product that will help prevent plaque and calculus build-up.

The Plaque Attackers® and Galileo Bone® are other excellent choices for the first three years of a dog's life. Their shapes make them interesting for the dog. As the dog chews on them, the solid polyurethane massages the gums which improves the blood circulation to the periodontal tissues. Projections on the chew devices increase the surface and are in contact with the tooth for more efficient cleaning. The unique shape and consistency prevent your dog from exerting excessive force on his own teeth or from breaking off pieces of the bone. If your dog is an aggressive chewer or weighs more than 55 pounds (25 kg), you should consider giving him a Nylabone®, the most durable chew product on the market.

Developing good chewing habits from the beginning is important to your Border Collie's well-being.

The Gumabones ®, made by the Nylabone Company, is constructed of strong polyurethane, which is softer than nylon. Less powerful chewers prefer the Gumabones® to the Nylabones®. A super option for your dog is the Hercules Bone®, a uniquely shaped bone named after the great Olympian for its exceptional strength. Like all Nylabone products, they are specially scented to make them attractive to your dog. Ask your veterinarian about these bones and he will validate the good doctor's prescription: Nylabones® not only give your dog a good chewing workout but also help to save your dog's teeth (and even his life, as it protects him from possible fatal periodontal diseases).

By the time dogs are four years old, 75% of them have periodontal disease. It is the most common infection in dogs. Yearly examinations by your veterinarian are essential to maintaining your dog's good health. If your veterinarian detects periodontal disease, he or she may recommend a prophylactic cleaning. To do a thorough cleaning, it will be necessary to put your dog under anesthesia. With modern gas anesthetics and monitoring equipment, the procedure is pretty safe. Your veterinarian will scale the teeth with an ultrasound scaler or hand instrument. This removes the calculus from the teeth. If there are calculus deposits below the gum line, the veterinarian will plane the roots to make them smooth. After all of the calculus has been removed, the teeth are polished with pumice in a polishing cup. If any medical or surgical treatment is needed, it is done at this time. The final step would be

fluoride treatment and your follow-up treatment at home. If the periodontal disease is advanced, the veterinarian may prescribe a medicated mouth rinse or antibiotics for use at home. Make sure your dog has safe, clean and attractive chew toys and treats. Chooz® treats are another way of using a consumable treat to help keep your dog's teeth clean.

Rawhide is the most popular of all materials for a dog to chew. This has never been good news to dog owners, because rawhide is inherently very dangerous for dogs. Thousands of dogs have died from rawhide, having swallowed the hide after it has become soft and mushy, only to cause stomach and intestinal blockage. A new rawhide product on the market has finally solved the problem of rawhide: molded Roar-Hide® from Nylabone®. These are composed of processed, cut up, and melted American rawhide injected into your dog's favorite shape: a dog bone. These dog-safe devices smell and taste like rawhide but don't break up. The ridges on the bones help to fight tartar build-up on the teeth and they last ten times longer than the usual rawhide chews.

The Nylabone® Frisbee™ is a must if you want to have fun with your Border Collie.
The trademark Frisbee is used under license from Mattel, Inc., California, USA.

Basic training will help your Border Collie develop good manners.

As your dog ages, professional examination and cleaning should become more frequent. The mouth should be inspected at least once a year. Your veterinarian may recommend visits every six months. In the geriatric patient, organs such as the heart, liver, and kidneys do not function as well as when they were young. Your veterinarian will probably want to test these organs' functions prior to using general anesthesia for dental cleaning. If your dog is a good chewer and you work closely with your veterinarian, your dog can keep all of its teeth all of its life. However, as your dog ages, his sense of smell, sight, and taste will diminish. He may not have the desire to chase, trap or chew his toys. He will also not have the energy to chew for long periods, as arthritis and periodontal disease make chewing painful. This will leave you with more responsibility for keeping his teeth clean and healthy. The dog that would not let you brush his teeth at one year of age, may let you brush his teeth now that he is ten years old.

If you train your dog with good chewing habits as a puppy, he will have healthier teeth throughout his life.

IDENTIFICATION and Finding the Lost Dog

There are several ways of identifying your dog. The old standby is a collar with dog license, rabies, and ID tags. Unfortunately collars have a way of being separated from the dog and tags fall off. We're not suggesting you shouldn't use a collar and tags. If they stay intact and on the dog, they are the quickest way of identification.

For several years owners have been tattooing their dogs. Some tattoos use a number with a registry. Here lies the problem because there are several registries to check. If you wish to tattoo, use your social security number. The humane shelters have the means to trace it. It is usually done on the inside of the rear thigh. The area is first shaved and numbed. There is no pain, although a few dogs do not like the buzzing sound. Occasionally tattooing is not legible and needs to be redone.

The newest method of identification is microchipping. The microchip is a computer chip that is no larger than a grain of rice. The veterinarian implants it by injection between the shoulder blades. The dog feels no discomfort. If your dog is lost and picked up by the humane society, they can trace you by scanning the microchip, which has its own code. Microchip

Make sure your Border Collie is in a securely fenced-in area if you must leave him alone for short periods of time.

scanners are friendly to other brands of microchips and their registries. The microchip comes with a dog tag saying the dog is microchipped. It is the safest way of identifying your dog.

Your Border Collie should wear a collar and identification tags at all times in case he becomes separated from you.

FINDING THE LOST DOG

I am sure you will agree that there would be little worse than losing your dog. Responsible pet owners rarely lose their dogs. They do not let their dogs run free because they don't want harm to come to them. Not only that but in most, if not all, states, countries, and cities there is a leash law.

The newest method of identification is microchipping. The microchip is a computer chip that is no bigger than a grain of rice.

Beware of fenced-in yards. They can be a hazard. Dogs find ways to

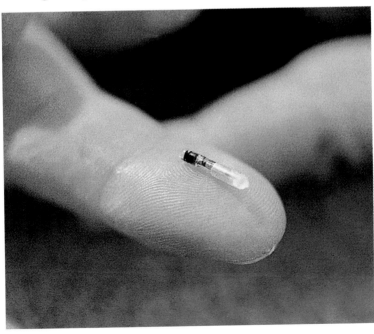

escape either over or under the fence. Another fast exit is through the gate that perhaps the neighbor's child left unlocked.

Below is a list that hopefully will be of help to you if you need it. Remember don't give up, keep looking. Your dog is worth your efforts.

Keep your Border Collie on lead at all times when out and about. This will ensure that he does not become separated from you.

1. Contact your neighbors and put flyers with a photo on it in their mailboxes. Information you should include would be the dog's name, breed, sex, color, age, source of identification, when your dog was last seen and where, and your name and phone numbers. It may be helpful to say the dog needs medical care. Offer a *reward*.

2. Check all local shelters daily. It is also possible for your dog to be picked up away from home and end up in an out-of-the-way shelter. Check these too. Go in person. It is not good enough to call. Most shelters are limited on the time they can hold dogs then they are put up for adoption or euthanized. There is the possibility that your dog will not make it to the shelter for several days. Your dog could have been wandering or someone may have tried to keep him.

3. Notify all local veterinarians. Call and send flyers.

4. Call your breeder. Frequently breeders are contacted when one of their breed is found.

5. Contact the rescue group for your breed.

6. Contact local schools—children may have seen your dog.

7. Post flyers at the schools, groceries, gas stations,

convenience stores, veterinary clinics, groomers and any other place that will allow them.

8. Advertise in the newspaper.

9. Advertise on the radio.

The Border Collie's urge to herd can also be applied to cars and bicycles—which can be very dangerous. Always leave him a in safe place when unsupervised.

TRAVELING with Your Border Collie

The earlier you start traveling with your new puppy or dog, the better. He needs to become accustomed to traveling. However, some dogs are nervous riders and become carsick easily. It is helpful if he starts with an empty stomach. Do not despair, as it will go better if you continue taking him with you on short fun rides. How would you feel if every time you rode in the car you stopped at the doctor's for an injection? You would soon dread that nasty car. Older dogs that tend to get carsick may have more of a problem adjusting to traveling. Those dogs that are having a serious problem may benefit from some medication prescribed by the veterinarian.

The versatile Border Collie is a "go anywhere" kind of dog. Blacktie Bailey, owned by Teresa Home, takes in the view.

Do give your dog a chance to relieve himself before getting into the car. It is a good idea to be prepared for a clean up with a leash, paper towels, bag and terry cloth towel.

The safest place for your dog is in a fiberglass crate, although close confinement can promote carsickness in some dogs. If your dog is nervous you can try letting him ride on the seat next to you or in someone's lap.

An alternative to the crate would be to use a car harness made for dogs and/or a safety strap attached to the harness or collar. Whatever you do, do not let your dog ride in the back of a pickup truck unless he is securely tied on a very short lead. I've seen trucks stop quickly and, even though the dog was tied, it fell out and was dragged.

If you take your Border Collie with you on vacation, bring along a few of his favorite toys to make him feel at home.

Another advantage of the crate is that it is a safe place to leave him if you need to run into the store. Otherwise you wouldn't be able to leave the windows down. Keep in mind that while many dogs are overly protective in their crates, this may not be enough to deter dognappers. In some states it is against the law to leave a dog in the car unattended.

Never leave a dog loose in the car wearing a collar and leash. More than one dog has killed himself by hanging. Do not let him put his head out an open window. Foreign debris can be blown into his eyes. When leaving your dog unattended in a car, consider the temperature. It can take less than five minutes to reach temperatures over 100 degrees Fahrenheit.

TRIPS

Perhaps you are taking a trip. Give consideration to what is best for your dog—traveling with you or boarding. When traveling by car, van or motor home, you need to think ahead about locking your vehicle. In all probability you have many valuables in the car and do not wish to leave it unlocked. Perhaps most valuable and not replaceable is your dog. Give thought to securing your vehicle and providing adequate

ventilation for him. Another consideration for you when traveling with your dog is medical problems that may arise and little inconveniences, such as exposure to external parasites. Some areas of the country are quite flea infested. You may want to carry flea spray with you. This is even a good idea when staying in motels. Quite possibly you are not the only occupant of the room. Unbelievably many motels and even hotels do allow canine guests, even some very first-class ones. Gaines Pet Foods Corporation publishes *Touring With Towser*, a directory of domestic hotels and motels that accommodate guests with dogs. Their address is Gaines TWT, PO Box 5700, Kankakee, IL, 60902. Call ahead to any motel that you may be considering and see if

If you accustom your Border Collie to car rides early, he will always be ready to hop in and tag along.

they accept pets. Sometimes it is necessary to pay a deposit against room damage. The management may feel reassured if you mention that your dog will be crated. If you do travel with your dog, take along plenty of baggies so that you can clean up after him. When we all do our share in cleaning up, we make it possible for motels to continue accepting our pets. As a matter of fact, you should practice cleaning up everywhere you take your dog.

Depending on where your are traveling, you may need an up-to-date health certificate issued by your veterinarian. It is good policy to take along your dog's medical information, which would include the name, address and phone number of your veterinarian, vaccination record, rabies certificate, and any medication he is taking.

AIR TRAVEL

When traveling by air, you need to contact the airlines to check their policy. Usually you have to make arrangements up to a couple of weeks in advance for traveling with your dog. The airlines require your dog to travel in an airline

Whether lounging at home or roughing it in the wild, the Border Collie is a very adaptable dog and can adjust to almost any situation.

approved fiberglass crate. Usually these can be purchased through the airlines but they are also readily available in most pet-supply stores. If your dog is not accustomed to a crate, then it is a good idea to get him acclimated to it before your trip. The day of the actual trip you should withhold water about one hour ahead of departure and no food for about 12 hours. The airlines generally have temperature restrictions, which do not allow pets to travel if it is either too cold or too hot. Frequently these restrictions are based on the temperatures at the departure and arrival airports. It's best to inquire about a health certificate. These usually need to be issued within ten days of departure. You should arrange for non-stop, direct flights and if a commuter plane should be involved, check to see if it will carry dogs. Some don't. The Humane Society of the United States has put together a tip sheet for airline traveling. You can receive a copy by sending a self-addressed stamped envelope to:

The Humane Society of the United States
Tip Sheet
2100 L Street NW
Washington, DC 20037.

Regulations differ for traveling outside of the country and are sometimes changed without notice. Well in advance you need to write or call the appropriate consulate or agricultural department for instructions. Some countries have lengthy quarantines (six months), and countries differ in their rabies vaccination requirements. For instance, it may have to be given at least 30 days ahead of your departure.

Do make sure your dog is wearing proper identification including your name, phone number and city. You never know when you might be in an accident and separated from your dog. Or your dog could be frightened and somehow manage to escape and run away.

Another suggestion would be to carry in-case-of-emergency instructions. These would include the address and phone number of a relative or friend, your veterinarian's name, address and phone number, and your dog's medical information.

BOARDING KENNELS

Perhaps you have decided that you need to board your dog. Your veterinarian can recommend a good boarding facility or possibly a pet sitter that will come to your house. It is customary for the boarding kennel to ask for proof of vaccination for the DHLPP, rabies and bordetella vaccine. The bordetella should have been given within six months of boarding. This is for your protection. If they do not ask for this proof I would not board at their kennel. Ask about flea control. Those dogs that suffer flea-bite allergy can get in trouble at a boarding kennel. Unfortunately boarding kennels are limited on how much they are able to do.

For more information on pet sitting, contact NAPPS:
National Association of Professional Pet Sitters
1200 G Street, NW
Suite 760
Washington, DC 20005.

Some pet clinics have technicians that pet sit and technicians that board clinic patients in their homes. This may be an alternative for you. Ask your veterinarian if they have an employee that can help you. There is a definite advantage of having a technician care for your dog, especially if your dog is on medication or is a senior citizen.

The Border Collie is such an accommodating dog, he can feel at home practically anywhere. This Border contemplates taking a dip.

You can write for a copy of *Traveling With Your Pet* from ASPCA, Education Department, 441 E. 92nd Street, New York, NY 10128.

BEHAVIOR and Canine Communication

S tudies of the human/animal bond point out the importance of the unique relationships that exist between people and their pets. Those of us who share our lives with pets understand the special part they play through companionship, service and protection. For many, the pet/owner bond goes beyond simple companionship; pets are often considered members of the family. A leading pet food manufacturer recently conducted a nationwide survey of pet owners to gauge just how important pets were in their lives. Here's what they found:

- 76 percent allow their pets to sleep on their beds
- 78 percent think of their pets as their children
- 84 percent display photos of their pets, mostly in their homes
- 84 percent think that their pets react to their own emotions
- 100 percent talk to their pets
- 97 percent think that their pets understand what they're saying

The bond between the Border Collie and his owner is a strong one.

Are you surprised?

Senior citizens show more concern for their own eating habits when they have the responsibility of feeding a dog. Seeing that their dog is routinely exercised encourages the owner to think of schedules that otherwise may seem

unimportant to the senior citizen. The older owner may be arthritic and feeling poorly but with responsibility for his dog he

Border Collies should be able to play with other dogs without displaying any fear, dominance, or aggression. These two seem to be getting along just fine.

has a reason to get up and get moving. It is a big plus if his dog is an attention seeker who will demand such from his owner.

Over the last couple of decades, it has been shown that pets relieve the stress of those who lead busy lives. Owning a pet has been known to lessen the occurrence of heart attack and stroke.

Many single folks thrive on the companionship of a dog. Lifestyles are very different from a long time ago, and today more individuals seek the single life. However, they receive fulfillment from owning a dog.

Most likely the majority of our dogs live in family environments. The companionship they provide is well worth the effort involved. In my opinion, every child should have the opportunity to have a family dog. Dogs teach responsibility through understanding their care, feelings and even respecting their life cycles. Frequently those children

The ultimate pet and companion, the Border Collie enriches the lives of his owners.

Dedicated owners consider their Border Collies valued members of the family. This quartet dutifully poses for a Christmas card.

who have not been exposed to dogs grow up afraid of dogs, which isn't good. Dogs sense timidity and some will take advantage of the situation.

Today more dogs are serving as service dogs. Since the origination of the Seeing Eye dogs years ago, we now have trained hearing dogs. Also dogs are trained to provide service for the handicapped and are able to perform many different tasks for their owners. Search and Rescue dogs, with their handlers, are sent throughout the world to assist in recovery of disaster victims. They are life savers.

Therapy dogs are very popular with nursing homes, and some hospitals even allow them to visit. The inhabitants truly look forward to their visits. They wanted and were allowed to have visiting dogs in their beds to hold and love.

Nationally there is a Pet Awareness Week to educate students and others about the value and basic care of our pets. Many countries take an even greater interest in their pets than

Americans do. In those countries the pets are allowed to accompany their owners into restaurants and shops, etc. In the U.S. this freedom is only available to our service dogs. Even so we think very highly of the human/animal bond.

CANINE BEHAVIOR

Canine behavior problems are the number-one reason for pet owners to dispose of their dogs, either through new homes, humane shelters or euthanasia. Unfortunately there are too many owners who are unwilling to devote the necessary time to properly train their dogs. On the other hand, there are those who not only are concerned about inherited health problems but are also aware of the dog's mental stability.

You may realize that a breed and his group relatives (i.e., sporting, hounds, etc.) show tendencies to behavioral characteristics. An experienced breeder can acquaint you with his breed's personality. Unfortunately many breeds are labeled with poor temperaments when actually the breed as a whole is not affected but only a small percentage of individuals within the breed.

Inheritance and environment contribute to the dog's behavior. Some naïve people suggest inbreeding as the cause of bad temperaments. Inbreeding only results in poor behavior if the ancestors carry the trait. If there are excellent temperaments behind the dogs, then inbreeding will promote good temperaments in the offspring. Did you ever consider that inbreeding is what sets the characteristics of a breed? A purebred dog is the end result of inbreeding. This does not spare the mixed-breed dog from the same problems. Mixed-breed dogs frequently are the offspring of purebred dogs.

The Border Collie is always ready for some fun and games.

Not too many decades ago most of our dogs led a different lifestyle than what is prevalent today. Usually mom stayed home so the dog had human companionship and someone to discipline it if needed. Not much was expected from the dog. Today's mom works and everyone's life is at a much faster pace.

The dog may have to adjust to being a "weekend" dog. The family is gone all day during the week, and the dog is left to his own devices for entertainment. Some dogs sleep all day waiting for their family to come home and others become wigwam

There are few things that escape the notice of the alert and curious Border Collie.

wreckers if given the opportunity. Crates do ensure the safety of the dog and the house. However, he could become a physical and

Without a doubt, the Border Collie is one of the most responsive herding breeds.

emotional cripple if he doesn't get enough exercise and attention. We still appreciate and want the companionship of our dogs although we expect more from them. In many cases we tend to forget dogs are just that—*dogs* not human beings.

SOCIALIZING AND TRAINING

Many prospective puppy buyers lack experience regarding the proper socialization and training needed to develop the type of pet we all desire. In the first 18 months, training does take some work. It is easier to start proper training before there is a problem that needs to be corrected.

The initial work begins with the breeder. The breeder should start socializing the puppy at five to six weeks of age and cannot let up. Human socializing is critical up through 12 weeks of age and likewise important during the following months. The litter should be left

A well-trained and well-socialized Border Collie is a joy to own and can accompany his owners anywhere.

together during the first few weeks but it is necessary to separate them by ten weeks of age. Leaving them together after that time will increase competition for litter dominance. If puppies are not socialized with people by 12 weeks of age, they will be timid in later life.

The eight- to ten-week age period is a fearful time for puppies. They need to be handled very gently around children and adults. There should be no harsh discipline during this time. Starting at 14 weeks of age, the puppy begins the juvenile period, which ends when he reaches sexual maturity around six to 14 months of age. During the juvenile period he needs to be introduced to strangers (adults, children and other dogs) on the home property. At sexual maturity he will begin to bark at strangers and become more protective. Males start to lift their legs to urinate but if you desire you can inhibit this behavior by walking your boy on leash away from trees, shrubs, fences, etc.

They say the Border Collie is no couch potato—but there are exceptions! This Border takes a snooze with her "dad."

147

Perhaps you are thinking about an older puppy. You need to inquire about the puppy's social experience. If he has lived in a kennel, he may have a hard time adjusting to people and environmental stimuli. Assuming he has had a good social upbringing, there are advantages to an older puppy.

Training includes puppy kindergarten and a minimum of one to two basic training classes. During these classes you will learn how to dominate your youngster. This is especially important if you own a large breed of dog. It is somewhat harder, if not nearly impossible, for some owners to be the Alpha figure when their dog towers over them. You will be taught how to properly restrain your dog. This concept is important. Again it puts you in the Alpha position. All dogs need to be restrained many times during their lives. Believe it or not, some of our worst offenders are the eight-week-old puppies that are brought to our clinic. They need to be gently restrained for a nail trim but the way they carry on you would think we were killing them. In comparison, their vaccination is a "piece of

Let your Border Collie meet as many different people as possible—especially children. The more people he meets, the better socialized he will become.

Your Border Collie will look to you, his owner, to be the leader of his pack.

cake." When we ask dogs to do something that is not agreeable to them, then their worst comes out. Life will be easier for your dog if you expose him at a young age to the necessities of life—proper behavior and restraint.

UNDERSTANDING THE DOG'S LANGUAGE

Most authorities agree that the dog is a descendent of the wolf. The dog and wolf have similar traits. For instance both are pack oriented and prefer not to be isolated for long periods of time. Another characteristic is that the dog, like the wolf, looks to the leader—Alpha—for direction. Both the wolf and the dog communicate through body language, not only within their pack but with outsiders.

Every pack has an Alpha figure. The dog looks to you, or should look to you, to be that leader. If your dog doesn't receive the proper training and guidance, he very well may replace you as Alpha. This would be a serious problem and is certainly a disservice to your dog.

Eye contact is one way the Alpha wolf keeps order within his pack. You are Alpha so you must establish eye contact with your puppy. Obviously your puppy will have to look at you. Practice eye contact even if you need to hold his head for five to ten seconds at a time. You can give him a treat as a reward. Make sure your eye contact is gentle and not threatening. Later, if he has been naughty, it is permissible to give him a long, penetrating look. There are some older dogs that never learned eye contact as puppies and cannot accept eye contact. You should avoid eye contact with these dogs since they feel threatened and will retaliate as such.

BODY LANGUAGE

The play bow, when the forequarters are down and the hindquarters are elevated, is an invitation to play. Puppies play fight, which helps them learn the acceptable limits of biting. This is necessary for later in their lives. Nevertheless, an owner may be falsely reassured by the playful nature of his dog's aggression. Playful aggression toward another dog or human may be an indication of serious aggression in the future. Owners should never play fight or play tug-of-war with any dog that is inclined to be dominant.

Signs of submission are:

1. Avoids eye contact.
2. Active submission—the dog crouches down, ears back and the tail is lowered.
3. Passive submission—the dog rolls on his side with his hindlegs in the air and frequently urinates.

Signs of dominance are:

1. Makes eye contact.

A loving and playful relationship with his dam and littermates is the first step to a well-socialized puppy.

2. Stands with ears up, tail up and the hair raised on his neck.
3. Shows dominance over another dog by standing at right angles over it.

Dominant dogs tend to behave in characteristic ways such as:
1. The dog may be unwilling to move from his place (i.e., reluctant to give up the sofa if the owner wants to sit there).
2. He may not part with toys or objects in his mouth and may show possessiveness with his food bowl.

Many people thrive on the devoted companionship that a Border Collie can provide. This Border accompanies his owners on a camping trip.

Does this look like the face of a mischief maker? Even a sweetheart like this can get into a lot of trouble if left unsupervised.

3. He may not respond quickly to commands.
4. He may be disagreeable for grooming and dislikes to be petted.

151

Dogs are popular because of their sociable nature. Those that have contact with humans during the first 12 weeks of life regard them as a member of their own species–their pack. All dogs have the potential for both dominant and submissive behavior. Only through experience and training do they learn to whom it is appropriate to show which behavior. Not all dogs are concerned with dominance but owners need to be aware of that potential. It is wise for the owner to establish his dominance early on.

A human can express dominance or submission toward a dog in the following ways:

The time you spend with your Border Collie will result in a close bond between dog and owner.

1. Meeting the dog's gaze signals dominance. Averting the gaze signals submission. If the dog growls or threatens, averting the gaze is the first avoiding action to take–it may prevent attack. It is important to establish eye contact in the puppy. The older dog that has not been exposed to eye contact may see it as a threat and will not be willing to submit.
2. Being taller than the dog signals dominance; being lower signals submission. This is why, when attempting to make friends with a strange dog or catch the runaway, one should kneel down to his level. Some owners see their dogs become dominant when allowed on the furniture or on the bed. Then he is at the owner's level.
3. An owner can gain dominance by ignoring all the dog's social initiatives. The owner pays attention to the dog only when he obeys a command.

No dog should be allowed to achieve dominant status over any adult or child. Ways of preventing are as follows:

1. Handle the puppy gently, especially during the three- to four-month period.
2. Let the children and adults handfeed him and teach him to take food without lunging or grabbing.
3. Do not allow him to chase children or joggers.
4. Do not allow him to jump on people or mount their legs. Even females may be inclined to mount. It is not only a male habit.
5. Do not allow him to growl for any reason.

6. Don't participate in wrestling or tug-of-war games.

7. Don't physically punish puppies for aggressive behavior. Restrain him from repeating the infraction and teach an alternative behavior. Dogs should earn everything they receive from their owners. This would include sitting to receive petting or treats, sitting before going out the door and sitting to receive the collar and leash. These types of exercises reinforce the owner's dominance.

Young children should never be left alone with a dog. It is important that children learn some basic obedience commands so they have some control over the dog. They will gain the respect of their dog.

FEAR

One of the most common problems dogs experience is being fearful. Some dogs are more afraid than others. On the lesser side, which is sometimes humorous to watch, dogs can be afraid of a strange object. They act silly when something is out of place in the house. We call his problem perceptive intelligence. He realizes the abnormal within his known environment. He does not react the same way in strange environments since he does not know what is normal.

In the end, there is nothing a Border Collie enjoys more than doing the work for which the breed was created.

A well-socialized Border Collie will not be hesitant to accept new places or people. On the more serious side is a fear of people. This can result in backing off, seeking his own space and saying "leave me alone" or it can result in an aggressive behavior that may lead to challenging the person. Respect that the dog wants to be left alone and give him time to come forward. If you approach the cornered dog, he may resort to snapping. If you leave him alone, he may decide to come forward, which should be rewarded with a treat.

Some dogs may initially be too fearful to take treats. In these cases it is helpful to make sure the dog hasn't eaten for about 24 hours. Being a little hungry encourages him to accept the treats, especially if they are of the "gourmet" variety.

155

Dogs can be afraid of numerous things, including loud noises and thunderstorms. Invariably the owner rewards (by comforting) the dog when it shows signs of fearfulness. When your dog is frightened, direct his attention to something else and act happy. Don't dwell on his fright.

AGGRESSION

Some different types of aggression are: predatory, defensive, dominant, possessive, protective, fear induced, noise provoked, "rage" syndrome (unprovoked aggression), maternal and aggression directed toward other dogs. Aggression is the most common behavioral problem encountered. Protective breeds are expected to be more aggressive than others but with the proper upbringing they can make very dependable companions. You need to be able to read your dog.

When properly trained and socialized, Border Collies are more than eager to please their masters.

Many factors contribute to aggression including genetics and environment. An improper environment, which may include the living conditions, lack of social life, excessive punishment, being attacked or frightened by an aggressive dog, etc., can all influence a dog's behavior. Even spoiling him and giving too much praise may be detrimental. Isolation and the lack of human contact or exposure to frequent teasing by children or adults also can ruin a good dog.

Lack of direction, fear, or confusion lead to aggression in those dogs that are so inclined. Any obedience exercise, even the sit and down, can direct the dog and overcome fear and/or confusion. Every dog should learn these commands as a youngster, and there should be periodic reinforcement.

Even the most well-tempered Border Collie can develop behavior problems, which is why it is important to be a firm but fair owner.

When a dog is showing signs of aggression, you should speak calmly (no screaming or hysterics) and firmly give a command that he understands, such as the sit. As soon as your dog obeys, you have assumed your dominant position. Aggression presents a problem because there may be danger to others. Sometimes it is an emotional issue. Owners may consciously or unconsciously encourage their dog's aggression. Other owners show responsibility by accepting the problem and taking measures to keep it under control. The owner is responsible for his dog's actions, and it is not wise to take a chance on someone being bitten, especially a child. Euthanasia is the solution for some owners and in severe cases this may be the best choice. However, few dogs are that dangerous and very few are that much of a threat to their owners. If caution is exercised and professional help is gained early on, most cases can be controlled.

Some authorities recommend feeding a lower protein (less than 20 percent) diet. They believe this can aid in reducing aggression. If the dog loses weight, then vegetable oil can be added. Veterinarians and behaviorists are having some success with pharmacology. In many cases treatment is possible and can improve the situation.

If you have done everything according to "the book" regarding training and socializing and are still having a behavior problem, don't procrastinate. It is important that the problem gets attention before it is out of hand. It is estimated that 20 percent of a veterinarian's time may be devoted to dealing with problems before they become so intolerable that the dog is separated from its home and owner. If your veterinarian isn't able to help, he should refer you to a behaviorist.

A Border Collie's toys can help keep him out of mischief.

RESOURCES

Border Collie Society of America
Contact: Sharon Ferguson
9002 Sovereign Rd, San Diego, CA , 92123-2341
www.bordercolliesociety.com

American Kennel Club
260 Madison Avenue
New York, New York 10016
or 5580 Centerview Drive
Raleigh, North Carolina 27606
919-233-3600
919-233-9767
www.akc.org

The Kennel Club
1 Clarges Street
Picadilly, London WIY 8AB, England

Canadian Kennel Club
100-89 Skyway Avenue
Etobicoke, Ontario , Canada
M9W6R4

The United Kennel Club, Inc.
100 E. Kilgore Road
Kalamazoo, Michigan 49002-5584
616-343-9020
www.ukcdogs.com

INDEX